The View from the Mountain
The Process of Destiny

Hewlette A.C. Pearson

Foreword by
Keith Duncan

PRESS

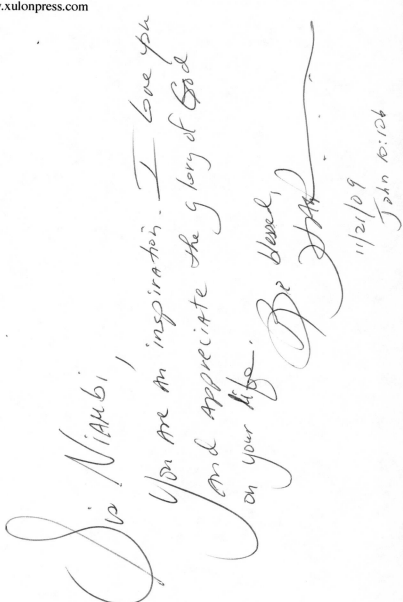

DEDICATION

To the loving memory of Myrtle B. French, who was a master teacher and one who lived a life of integrity with great fortitude. I stumble sometime as I try to walk in her shoes. Her mantle is now mine.

TABLE OF CONTENTS

ACKNOWLEDGEMENTS

To those who walked with me along the way...

I am truly blessed with the best, most supportive, loving and giving family in the whole world—The Pearsons! Thanks Mom & Dad (Gretel & Felix), Daniel & Josephine, Aldean I & Julianne†, Glendon & Itari, and my wonderful nieces and nephews: Devon, Gabriel, Alayna, Aldean II, Jasmine, and Daniel Jr. You bring much joy to my heart. I love you all so very much.

Auntie Locketta & Uncle Joseph, and cousins LaToya, Ann Marie, & Ian (The Newmans), thanks for believing in me.

My Godchildren: Kaleb, Bryanna, and Mikayla—thank you for being my little rays of sunshine and for telling me, "God loves you, Auntie Hewie," through your smiles, hugs, and kisses.

June Sutherland, you are a dear friend who went through much just to "walk" with me. You are more than I deserve. Without you pushing me, this book would still be a thought. Thanks for your unconditional love and being a "forever" friend.

Winston & Juliet Maxwell, true friends you are. You gave out of your nothing and stood by me through thick and thin. God will reward you for it.

Patela & Delroy Oakley, thank you for your friendship and for pouring into my life in such a wonderful way. I am still amazed, truly.

Penelope "Lisa" Griffith, thanks for helping me to maintain a proper balance during the "dark times." God is going to bless you for standing in the gap. You are an "on time" friend. Here's to you and the "church in the den."

Donna James, thanks for the best chicken soup ever! You were there when I needed you most. Girl, your promise is coming!

Rhoda Blackwood, thanks for your unselfish acts of love. Those great home cooked meals hit the spot. Keep on cooking and giving. You'll always entertain angels unaware. Your heart is what He sees.

Sylvia Griffith, you are a gift from the Father. I appreciate your love and support of me. Your works will precede you into the kingdom of God.

Gerald and Patricia Nathe, thank you so very much for showing just how much I mean to you. Your kind acts of love are appreciated, and you'll always be my "special mom & dad."

Jerome and LaTonya Pritchett, thank you for encouraging me as I went through my storm. LaTonya, thanks for teaching me how to say a very important word—"No!"

Rachel Carter, thanks for helping me see that my gift can bless others. You're a God-send and an encourager.

Jill M. Morris, thank you for your honesty and friendship. Your tenacious spirit inspires me.

Dr. Rosemarie Downer, thanks for helping to meet a need in the right season. You helped to fill the gap between loss and gain.

Allo Peterkin, thank you for being obedient to the voice of God and giving me those prophetic words. Your constant prayer and support are appreciated.

Marjorie Carson, thanks for sharing what was on God's heart regarding me. It was then I realized how much He truly loves me. Continue to walk in your prophetic calling.

Frankie Montgomery, you saw it before many did. Thank you for letting me know that God has called me to something greater—ministry to the nations.

Georgia Jackson, Marshall & Beverly Pulliam, Queenie Carson, Hilret & Michael Passmore, Nedra Clark ("Twin,"), Lonnell & Nichole Pritchett, JoAnne Carson, Kathy Dessosow, Errol & Merline Mowatt, Minnie Turner, Antoinette Dickerson, Gabriel and Michelle Trofort, Jacqueline Allen, Philip Gordon, Marcia Sutherland, Olivia Hird, Enez Burrell, Stephen & Elaine French, Wanda Myers, Elizabeth Hawkins, and Samuel & Susan Carson—thank you for being my "cheerleaders." Your cheers still move heaven.

Thanks to Ann Turk, Rebecca Bertram, Rosa Caldera, Amy Coleman, Beth DuBoff, Janice DeHaven, Debra Coldsmith, and Sandra Williams for believing in and inspiring me to pursue my dreams.

Patricia Fingal, the best hairstylist in the world, thanks for pouring into my life in such a unique way. I look beautiful every time I step out of your salon. I appreciate your friendship and ministry.

Audrey Thomas, what can I say that will sum up just how much I admire you? You are the consummate attorney who seeks out the best for others. Your relationship with God is a testament to your knowing and listening to His voice. Continue to follow His lead.

Tamara Fingal, you are such a wonderful mentee that I enjoy guiding through life's maze. Your gifts to the body of Christ will always move heaven. By the way, thanks for keeping me up to date on the latest slang, fashion and music. Sing, girl! Sing!

Evangelist Tracy Gibson, thank you for being a woman of faith and much creativity. It's great having you as a sister in ministry. Your friendship means a lot to me.

Sharon Prather, Tasha Green, Joyce Prempeh, Esther Gyermeh, Kimberly Fry, Agnes Goodrich, and Dr. Kimberly Keys—thank you for godly advice and support during my first year in seminary. Regent University will never be the same because of us.

FOREWORD

A side from knowing Jesus Christ, and Him crucified, buried yet raised from the dead, and coming back for His saints, the second and greatest need for a person to discover is his purpose in life.

In today's society, we have forgotten that life is about the fulfillment of one's destiny. We have failed to communicate from one generation to the next the significance of life. We have modeled the importance of fitting in to a culture rather than being a radical that would go against the pop culture and become a world changer. Because of this we have seen such a decline in our society. Why? Because so many have failed to discover their purpose, much less walk it out in life. Yet, there is still hope!

We must be the radicals that will rise up and speak to this society and culture with the message not only of Christ, but also that every person has a specific purpose and destiny to fulfill that will impact this society and will aid in the advancement of the Kingdom of Heaven. We must understand that salvation is the starting point to our lives and that God has specific plans and purposes for us to accomplish.

It all begins with the discovery of one's purpose. This has to be the starting place for all, and this can only be found while in the presence of God. Ephesians 2:10 says, "For we are His workmanship, created in Christ Jesus for good works, which God prepared beforehand that we should walk in them." We know that it is by grace that man is saved and not of works lest any man should boast, but James also indicates that faith without works is dead. The problem with today's society is that the message has ended at the foot of the cross, and there has not been a clear rally cry for these believers to become world changers. Salvation is merely the beginning point of the plan that God has purposed for our lives. The salvation experience is designed to automatically segue into the next step of life's journey, and that next phase is the development phase.

This development stage is much like the gestation period experienced by women who are pregnant. It is a time when so many changes are taking place. It is a time when a plethora of emotions are experienced, but it is a time that is critical for the growth and development of that which is contained within the womb of the woman, and it is in this phase where your purpose begins its growth as well—in the womb of destiny.

In this book, Hewlette Pearson will become transparent as she shares the steps of her journey in this development stage of purpose. You will laugh with her, and even find yourself shedding tears as she tells of the journey to her destiny. You will discover that amidst some of the most critical, and even life threatening of circumstances, your destiny and purpose will see you through to the other side as long as you keep your eyes upon the Master conductor to this symphony of life—Jesus Christ.

Now is the time to take the Kingdom, and now is the time to posses our land! When you do, you will look back across the great times of distress, failures, and the many negative opinions of man that were spoken over you while you were pregnant with your purpose, and you will remember the pain of those wounds no more. Why? Because you have birthed that which you have been carrying within your spiritual womb and you can now see, "The View from the Mountain."

Keith Duncan †
His Call Ministries
P.O. Box 49307
Charlotte, N.C. 28277
803.547.2210
www.HisCall.org

INTRODUCTION

WHAT IS THIS BOOK ABOUT ANYWAY?

Have you ever been through situations where you felt like Job? Okay, you may not have lost all your children. Your personal material possessions may all still be intact. Your business may never have failed. You may not have talked to God with the expectation of getting an answer back and none is returned. And to top it off, your spouse of some years may not have looked you in the eyes and said, "Curse God and die."

Oh yes, I forgot. You may not have had three friends that judged you in your time of agony and loss and then blamed you for all the bad things that were happening. Talking about hell on earth! Well, you may not have experienced that entire drama, but it sure feels like it when you're going through, doesn't it? Probably if Job were here today, we would likely give him a high-five and say, "Man, I know what you've been through. I can relate!"

No struggle seems easy when you are in the thick of it. No hurdle in your way lies down and says, "Ok, come on, I'll make it easy for you." No disappointment flails its arms in the air to alert you of its coming. No pain eases at the first beat of the heart or the slightest twitch of the body. And no joy cheers at the entrance of each morning to reassure you that you'll not shed another tear.

But this I am sure of without a shadow of a doubt: no struggle, no hurdle, no disappointment, and no pain can ever change the fact that God is God and very much in control! He is sovereign. It is because of this fact that I know He will bring you out of any and every struggle, hurdle, disappointment, and pain you are experiencing. You are not alone! Hold on and embrace the Divine Company that is with you.

Surely He is with us, this I know. Every breath we take, every mistake we make, each time we feel like "throwing in the towel," and every time we give Him a soft and gentle whisper, "I love you," He is right there. Such a relationship creates a truer reality of who we are and reassures us that His divine hand is upon our lives.

It is quite easy at times to judge God according to how we feel or what situations we find ourselves in. We may say — "God doesn't love me" — because He doesn't answer the prayer we think is most urgent. We may get angry because He did not come through on the plan we formulated without His input. And we may probably go as far to say, "He doesn't care about me," because someone rejected us or walked out on a relationship. But is it fair to paint a portrait of God with the same brush and colors of our situation? Is it fair to expect Him to be constant when we vacillate between emotions and intellect, between truth and falsehood?

Believe me I would love to say no, but as a result of my walk with the Lord I have come to realize that my concept of Him is measured sharply by my experience with Him. Good or bad, we create images of what a person is like based upon what occurs in the relationship. The image becomes sharper and clearer as the experiences teach us who we are and who He TRULY is. He is God Almighty, All-knowing, All-seeing, and All-powerful. Malachi 3:6a says, *"For I am the Lord, I change not.* " In this I find it is fair for me to expect Him to be there when no one else is, to secure and protect me, to love and embrace me, to understand why I mess up, to be everything I expect a god of His magnitude and power to be, and to be constant in all these and more. Does this mean I live and do what I want? No, it does not, but it places me in a correct posture—a servant.

Interestingly enough, all this expectation I have of God amounts to basically only one thing—Faith. Because I expect Him to be this and more to me, He creates and orchestrates situations in my life to expose, amplify, and reveal those attributes of Himself. And in the brightness of this revelation, I see who I truly am. What a mighty God He is!

Because our walk with God is one of faith, we sometimes find that this whole walking experience, according to His leading, is costly. An old Jamaican proverb says, *"Talk is cheap, but living is expensive."* Living what we sing and read about in the Bible does not add up as easily as one plus one.

There are some experiences in life that can cause subtraction rather than addition; there are even times when we may experience division. But we can be assured that the Master Mathematician is in control and He does not count numbers; He makes numbers count. It is not how many struggles we have been through that matter; it is what the struggles have worked out in us. This is the *process of destiny.*

Centuries ago, Christ, the incarnate Son of God, gave up His regality to put on humanity. He began and ended His journey with one thing in mind—you and I. No rejection, abuse, lie, anger, betrayal, disbelief, or wrath could keep Him away from His immediate destiny—a hill of shame, disgrace, ridicule, anguish, pain, and death.

No matter the struggle, no matter the ignominy of His death, Christ did it all just for us. When He died, was buried, and rose gloriously triumphant from the dead, He moved the starting line of the race further up towards the finish line. As we walk with the Lord now, we begin the journey where He finished His—on the mountain.

The View from the Mountain is not an exhaustive history of chronicled struggles and triumphs. No, for if it were your hands would tire quite easily from the voluminous text. Rather, it is about experiences encountered while making my way up to other levels on the mountain and lessons learned on the journey toward destiny. Have I reached the top yet? Of course not! The perspective from which I give my story is nestled somewhere in between heaven and earth. I am taken up at times by the sheer essence of glory and knocked back into reality by the "experience" brush of humanity.

So as you read, please know that I write to encourage you to keep on walking, climbing. I become transparent so that you will know God feels and understands your pain. I hold things back so you will stay focused on what really matters—you. I share joys and spurts of laughter to portray reality. And I occasionally reflect to push you in the right direction—upward.

CHAPTER ONE

DATING, COURTING, AND KNOWING: EXPERIENCING GOD

"Sometimes I think I understand everything...
Then I regain consciousness."
—Ashleigh Brilliant

God. Who is God? As a child my curiosity seemed at its peak. I wondered why God's name was called so much. How come He never showed up when people called Him? There were times I felt that He would walk through the door any minute, but I just never saw Him. In church I heard "God." At home I heard "God." And at school I heard "God," but often with an expletive following close behind.

Calling God's name was not enough. Jesus Christ was following a close second. No disrespect intended, but as a child that name only meant one thing to me—the invisible man. We were taught never to take His name in vain, and so it seemed strange to me how His name was constantly being uttered throughout the church services. Many of the older women in church would raise their hand to their mouth, suck their teeth, and move their torso from one side to the next while saying "Jesus." It seemed as if they were mad at somebody else, but called His name instead. Surely they must have been aware of the rule also.

DATING...

Part of my curiosity about God was laid to rest when I received Christ as my personal Savior at the age of eleven. It was like going out on my first date. My nerves were a wreck! Every testimony service before that auspicious day — baptism celebration — I knew certain eyes were upon me in expectation of my getting up and testifying. It was as if they were testing my sincerity on wanting to be baptized. Did I want to testify to prove I was a worthy candidate for baptism? No, but I had no other choice. The older saints' eyes latched onto my body, dragged me up from my seat, and stood me upright, or so it seemed as their piercing eyes proved to be much more than a concerned stare.

If the older saints' eyes were not enough to move me, it would only take the move of one of my peers testifying to do the trick. Eyes would roll and teeth would hiss when one of us stood up first. It was as if all the rest of us were saying, "Oh man, what she go and do that for? Now I have to get up and testify. Gosh!"

There were times that standing seemed more a punishment than the terror of actually testifying. Why? Well, the times I stood and had to wait my turn felt like years had passed by before the person officiating acknowledged my presence on the floor. It felt like everyone waited in anticipation to see what would come from this young person's mouth. But it would always be the same thing, "Thank the Lord for waking me up this morning in my right mind. Thank the Lord for taking me on the busy highway and bringing me home safely. Those who know the *words* of prayer, please pray my strength in the Lord."

Whew! I did it. It was now somebody else's turn to turn blue. Interestingly enough, it was not until I got older that I found out that it was not, "Those who know the *words* of prayer..." rather it is "Those who know the *worth* of prayer..." Don't ask me where we got it from; we just mimicked what the old folks said. I don't even think they realized that I had made a mistake. I think they were just absorbed by the fact that the young people were eager to show they loved the Lord and wanted to testify of His goodness.

However, after a few weeks, my Mom got tired of the repetitious testimony. She cornered me and my brothers one day at home and asked,

"What highway have you been on?"

We looked at each other and wondered what she was talking about, but we dared not ask it.

"I just asked you a question, what highway have you been on?" she asked again.

Knowing what I know now, I would have probably said with a question in my voice,

"I'm walking up the King's highway?"

But then again, I would probably be wearing dentures right about now. We truly did not know what our Mom was talking about. But, we knew somehow she had the answer. It was surely in our best interest to stay quiet and respectful.

We just stood there with big question marks on our foreheads. Then suddenly, with a sternness that felt like a belt was hovering very close by, my Mom said,

"If I hear you testify about 'keeping you on the busy highway' again, you will have to answer to me," she exclaimed.

My Mom always made sense even when she didn't. She just had the "power" to let us see things the way she did. So yes indeed, she always made sense. Truly, we had never been on any highway. We only went to school, home, and church. No highway was involved in any of those areas we traveled. But because that was the "in" testimony at the time, all the young people followed the older saints' "powerful" orations.

Getting a chance to really date this "Guy" (no disrespect intended) at first seemed like an uphill battle. It was more than just testifying; that just did not do the trick. I did not know Jesus like the older people did. Seeing everybody around me talking about how great He was moved me to experience Him for myself.

Our baptism was glorious. Over a hundred people had gathered in the church we rented to witness this solemn, yet electrifying event. It was the largest baptism my church had ever had. We were all dressed in white, all thirteen of us, and we stood in a row across the front of the church for everyone to see us. I remember I had on a white pillbox-type hat, white blouse and skirt, white pantyhose, and black shoes. Each of us had to say something before we were taken to change into our baptismal attire.

No, I didn't do it; at least not this time. The busy highway testimony just did not come to me that day. Maybe my Mom scared it out of me, but I would rather think that the step I was about to make called for something from deep within me. I remember fighting back the tears as the microphone was pushed in front of my face, "I just want to say that I love Jesus, and I want to live a holy life just for Him."

I remember saying it with a tremble in my voice. I don't remember the response of the crowd or the testimony of the others. At that moment, it seemed as if I were standing on a white-sanded beach alone, watching the waves flow in, listening to the wind howl the words, "I love you, too."

The applause of the congregation snapped me back to reality. I remember being escorted to the "ready" room. There was not much talking; I think we were all just a little scared. Scared of the chilly water and what would happen if they didn't hold our noses just right.

COURTING...

Getting the Holy Spirit was no joke! I come from a Pentecostal background and there were two words the young people dreaded to hear, but knew would come around at least once a month—tarrying service. Just writing those two words caused chill bumps to arise on my arms and pushed me, at warp speed, back to one of those services.

But before I tell you about it, I want you to know that I did receive the Holy Spirit at the age of fourteen and spoke in "elegant" tongues for several minutes. Yes, receiving the gift of the Holy Spirit brought me closer to my "Date;" we really started to go "steady." The more I found out about Him, the more my spirit yearned to know more.

Remember that tarrying service I promised I would tell you about? Well, here it goes. It was a Saturday evening designated just for tarrying service. All the young people gathered unwillingly and in a melancholy manner. It was just not something we looked forward to having. We knew which songs would make us cry; we knew which songs would just push us to the edge of not trying.

I won't mention it here in fear of disappointing the writers, but one song in particular did not sit well with any of us. If you were to wake up any of my friends from back then at 2 o'clock in the morning and ask them to sing the "dreaded" tarrying song, they would sing it without thinking twice. What made it even worse was the older saints just loved singing it. Why? I don't know.

Couldn't they sense it in the Spirit that we just "hated" the song? You could be on the "line" (this means right at the point of getting the Holy Spirit) and as you'd begin to make progress, some "warrior" (an older saint) would begin to bellow out a couple bars of that song. Just the first bar alone would knock you right back to the point where you started saying, "Jesus, Jesus, Jesus...," at a fast pace all over again.

Well the service was on its way. We were admonished by the saints and encouraged to lay it all before the feet of Jesus. "Ask Him to forgive you of all your sins, big sins and little sins, even the ones you don't know about," they would tell us.

I didn't have any big sins, and I surely couldn't tell Him about the ones I didn't know I had committed. So I ventured on moving meticulously through the annals of my brief history to scour my brain to see what "little" sins I had done. It was not hard to do as it was a private undertaking. No one was present in my mind to view my secrets, nor the little sins from which I had forgotten to ask of God for forgiveness.

Taking change from my Mom's purse to buy candy for my friends was on the top of my list. Oh yeah and sneaking in their bedroom while they were out to watch television came in at a close second to lying about taking a bath. Basically, all I had done was just wet the tub and ran the water over my washcloth so it appeared to have been used to wash my body. Let me stop you before you go there.

The wetting the bath and washcloth was one of those "old" sins that I had to scour my mind for. That happened when I was between the ages of nine and eleven. Look, I wasn't the only one either. My brothers were in cahoots with me too. It's a funny story, but I think I'll write about it in my next book.

Now there…refocus your mind to the tarrying story. The service started getting "hot." The songs were right on point; some of us began to really feel the need to get filled with the Spirit. You could hear the occasional sob, the moan, and occasional "Jesus!" outburst from among the small group of us gathered around the altar. The prayer warriors meandered their way through the crowd to check to see if we were on the "line" (close to the point of speaking in tongues). They would put their ear to our head right where it rested on our arms by our elbows and say, "Come on. Get on the line! Tell Him everything!"

Some would come and encourage us by singing or rubbing our backs. Others would come and put tissue by your knee or wipe your nose if they thought something was happening. Boy what a scene. But we knew we had to do it or we would be there for a lo-o-o-o-ong time.

A couple of the prayer warriors had gathered around one of the young girls in the group and was working with her. She was crying and screaming for Jesus. She called on Him like He was a thousand miles away; we all did for that matter and hoped it would be that evening He would show up to fill us with the Holy Spirit. Breaking the soft silent sobs with her scream and outward cries for Jesus did the rest of us in.

Like the testimony, the same was true for the tarrying service. If one person started to cry out and openly show visible signs of tears and mucous, then the race was on to see who would be next. We all started to moan and sob louder. When tears would not naturally flow, we made them ourselves.

On one particular occasion, it was pretty hard for me to cry. I tried to cry while picturing Jesus hanging on the cross with nails in His feet and hands. I could fake the cry and screams for Jesus, but no matter how hard I tried not enough tears would formulate to trickle down my face as a sign that I was near or getting close to being on the "line." "Forget it," I said to myself after the tears just would not come.

But, being the bright twelve year-old I was, I decided to make my tears roll like a river or at least appear to do so. I mustered up enough saliva as I could, placed my forefinger in my mouth, retrieved as much liquid I could get without attracting any attention to what I was doing, and poured on the tears. I even lifted my head while crying for Jesus so that the prayer warriors could see that there were visible tears and that I was on the "line" now. Some came by and said,

"See Jesus!"
And others said,
"Hold on! Just keep holding on!"
And then right behind her someone would say,
"Let go! Just let go!"
Confused? No, I knew exactly what they meant. It was their way of saying your time is here, just see Him doing exactly what you want Him to do for you.

I have learned that although as tiring as it may have been, such services worked out the mess in me. It got me thinking about how I should live my life in earnest expectation of Him coming to me at anytime (not just during tarrying service) to fill me with His precious presence. Whenever we remembered that a tarrying service was taking place the next weekend, we lived our life that week as if it were our last. Everything we did was predicated on the fact that the service we disliked was coming, but we wanted all that it had to offer.

KNOWING...

As a result of that experience, I began to learn more about how I should live my life—waiting for Him to show up at any minute to bless me. I began to move from going steady with Jesus to knowing Him a little more intimately. I found Him to be more than what I heard the older saints talk about. I'm much older now, and I've come to the realization that some of the things they did with us was founded upon what they were taught and what they experienced themselves. They only gave us their best with what they knew to do.

No one got hurt from tarrying before the Lord. The environment was clean and anointed. It allowed the Holy Spirit to flow on His own accord. Because I did not understand that then, I struggled with forcing Him to come into "this" temple. He did come, but only at the point where I learned to praise Him for the gift rather than beg Him for it.

My walk with the Lord has been "splendifferent!" That is a word that Elder Samuel Carson, Sr., coined several years ago. It's been splendid, yet different. You know when something looks ugly or is not done in the best manner and someone asks your opinion on it? Well, instead of saying, "My goodness, that's horrible," you say, "Now that's different!"

Well, my walk with the Lord has been marvelous and "different." Not that it has been horrible. No, not HORRIBLE, but my walk has been rocky at times and there has been hurt and pain. There are just some things that I'd never imagined happening to me, especially messes God chose not to spare me from though He knew I was going to walk right into them. But, He's a keeper! I mean He's the kind of God I want to be attached to for the rest of my life. Yes! I'm getting to know Him better every day.

I know my relationship with Him has its ups and downs, but when we get to talking about it and seeing the lessons learned and pits avoided, it makes me cling closer to Him, close enough to whisper, "Wow! That was a close one." Or, "Dad, I truly love you." And sometimes, "Ooops! Sorry for not being obedient."

Remember the busy highway testimony? Well, I have my own now.

Lord, I thank you for loving me beyond measure, for the times You stepped in and blocked the path to destruction. I bless Your name for the many times You held my hand through the storm and the times You kept me calm in the storm.

I truly bless and extol my God for being greater than my problems, more beautiful than a clear summer day, ever faithful and true, trustworthy and loving, and stronger than the power of sin.

I even thank You for the times You did not answer some of my prayers. I look back and see that many of

*them were selfish and cowardice. Some of the things
I asked for were things You gave me the power to
do myself. You are the Master Teacher, and I am
learning from You each day. I say I thank God for His
manifold blessings toward me. It could have been the
other way, but God...*

I could have died many times over, but God...

I could have been comatose, but God...

*I could be locked up in a mental institution, but
God...*

*Hallelujah! I could have been a prostitute, but
God...*

I could have been a homosexual, but God...

*Praise His Name! I could have been a murderer,
a fornicator, a thief, a drug addict, an alcoholic, a
liar, or many other things, but God...!*

*Hallelujah! Glory be to God! I thank Him for the
power to live a victorious life. I bless His name for
the Holy Spirit who guides and protects me. I honor
Him for the life of integrity that He has afforded me
to live. I praise Him for the sense of humor He has
given me to bring laughter to the hearts of others.
I love Him for the costly anointing that is flowing
through me. And I worship His majesty for the
glimpse of His glory.*

*Many friends have come and gone, many guys
have spoken sweet words, but none can be compared
to the awesome friendship and embrace I experience
being His child and a worshiper in His presence.
Bless the Lord!*

*I also bless the Lord for you as you are using
your precious time to read this book. May you feel
His special love in your heart as you gain insight
from my experiences. May the smiles that come to
your face as a result of my stories bring healing in*

the areas needed. And may the "reflection on lessons learned" help you on your journey.

Saints and friends, I don't mean to take up too much time with you in this chapter, but..."When I think of the goodness of Jesus, and all He has done for me, my soul cries out, Hallelujah! Thank God for saving me." Those of you, who know the worth of prayer, please pray my strength in the Lord. Amen!

Now that's a testimony!

CHAPTER TWO

A LOST OPPORTUNITY

*"Life is short and the days ahead are uncertain,
so make a difference today."*
—H.A. Pearson

America. What a great land! Not knowing too much about Yankee Doodle coming into town, the Pilgrims landing at Plymouth Rock, the Pony Express, or the great battle at Bull Run did not alarm my teachers as they knew I was not the typical American Yankee. A Jamaican by birth and an American by naturalization, I fought long and hard to assimilate both in attitude and speech. It did not work, though, as I stood out like a sore thumb waiting to become one again with the rest of the hand. My parents could not afford to dress us up in the latest fashions, so we wore what were available—fashions from the thrift shop or homemade fashions by Mom.

As a child, I hated growing up in America my first few years. The kids were so mean and devious. My brothers and I underwent so much cruelty at fellow classmates' hands that I think I may be scarred for life. Everyday I went to school I was teased, poked, laughed at, scorned, and threatened. I even remember a song my classmates made up about me and one of my brothers when I was in 4th grade. Every time they saw us walking in the hallways, they would begin to sing it. Sing it they did while gyrating their adolescent bodies in sundry motions. Some told me to my face that I was from the jungles of Africa and that I wore no clothes over there.

"Do you guys still live in huts?" one classmate asked. Did I answer? Most definitely not! I relished the little bit of sanity I was allowed to maintain in their presence. I would just squeeze my eyes tight and hope they would just go away, very far away.

Elementary school in the late 70s was vicious. But, by the time I reached middle school things began to simmer down some. My entourage of friends was comprised of nerds, rejects, and goofballs; at least that's what they called us. To me, however, we were the greatest of pals—intelligent, studious, creative, humorous, and friendly. We were always the ones getting the awards at school assembly times. We knew just how to get back at those "perfect" ones.

I had a wonderful friend named Calista Njoku. She came here from Nigeria at a very young age. You wouldn't have thought she was an African unless you'd heard her last name. She did not have a strong accent like me. As a matter of fact, there wasn't one; at least I didn't hear it. There simply were no outward visible signs revealing that the United States of America was not her land of birth.

When we graduated from middle school, we all decided (the nerds, rejects, and goofballs) to go to the same high school—Calvin Coolidge Senior High. It was a large school with long hallways and a big football field. Most of us tried to stick together as best we could, but each quarter brought with it a different set of classes. We were beginning to make choices that would affect our future. I ventured towards the liberal arts classes and Calista towards business and management.

College was not a question for us. Both our parents were from strict backgrounds. They expected their children to achieve more than what they were able to do with their limited resources, so Calista and I set our ambitions high. We began sending out applications to the "good schools" like Spellman College and Chicago, Howard, Temple, George Washington, American, and Georgetown Universities.

Now we both knew we had about as much chance to get into those schools as an ice cube in ninety-five degree weather sitting in a McDonald's cup; we didn't even have the money to attend. Our grades were competitive, but our SAT scores were damaging to our track records; moreover, our parents just did not have the bundle of cash needed to finance such a formidable venture.

Calista and I ended up at our state (city) university—the University of the District of Columbia—also affectionately known as the "University of Distinguished Colleagues." A multitude of diplomats and foreign students attended the school, or so it seemed.

As we matriculated through college, Calista and I grew apart. I remember looking for her my second semester and was told she was working at a bank. I would occasionally see her at the bank in my neighborhood and would exchange cordialities. We even got a few opportunities to ask each other about old friends and chat about what was going on in our lives.

After a couple years went by, I did not see Calista anymore. It didn't bother me as much being that I knew how to get in touch with her if I needed to. We just took different paths that lead us away from each other. We still lived in the same neighborhood for a while, but we just didn't take the time to visit one another.

Nine years quickly passed by since I had last spoken with Calista. I was still living at home, but she had moved out of the neighborhood. I was busy following my dreams, traveling, singing with a recording choir, and doing undercover investigative work. One day I came home from work and was greeted by a familiar voice on my answering machine. It was Calista calling to see how I was and asking to set a time and place for us to meet. I was so excited about the message that I ran downstairs, hollered for my Mom who was sitting on the porch outside, and said, "Mom, guess what? Remember Calista, my classmate? I just received a message on my machine from her."

Mom seemed as excited as I was to hear from Calista and encouraged me to follow up on the call. I began to reminisce right there and then, telling my mother about our antics and how we carried on in Home Economics class, made up songs about our teachers, and whispered about the boys we secretly liked.

When I returned Calista's call, I was greeted by the voice of a little boy (and Calista's voice coaching him in the background) on her answering machine. I responded, "Calista, Oh my goodness! It's so great to hear from you. Who is the little man on the machine? Please call me back as soon as you get this message."

She called back, but my answering service greeted her again. She revealed that the little voice I had heard on the machine was her 4-year-old son. I smiled when I heard it and looked forward to our talking and meeting in person.

This phone tag relay went on for a week or two. It eventually got to the point where neither one of us was calling anymore. I was too busy anyway and the excitement that initially fueled my desire to talk to and meet with Calista waned over time.

About three weeks after the last answering machine tag relay, I received a call. It was a call from Calista's eldest sister. I did not make much of it at first as I thought she was only making the call for Calista who would soon come to the phone. But that was not the case.

"Calista is dead, Hewlette. I'm calling you to let you know and to ask for your help," she continued.

"Hello! Hello! Hewlette, are you there?" she kept saying.

I felt like I was in a trance, spinning around in a world of silence and void, reliving all the answering machine messages we left for each other. I snapped out of it in time to answer her sister.

"Okay, sure. Just let me know what you need," I whispered with a sad tone.

I sat on the edge of my bed with tears running down my face and arms limp to my sides. I gazed into the emptiness that now engulfed my bedroom. I began to imagine the struggle she experienced—fighting for air while trying to gain enough strength to get up from the floor. As these thoughts rushed through my mind, it was as if every pore in my skin was open waiting for the signal to scream.

"Calista is dead?" I asked myself. I knew the answer, but I was asking much more than that. I was asking, "Why didn't we talk? Why didn't we meet? Why wasn't I given the opportunity to meet your son? Why didn't you get the chance to see me? Why didn't I get the chance to see you?"

Calista died of an asthma attack in front of her son. I was told that she called 911, but did not have the strength to talk to the operator. The paramedics came and tried their best to revive her, but nothing worked. It was too late.

It was too late for me too. I lost a wonderful friend and the opportunity to share God's love, His arms, His smile, His warmth, His care, and His touch. I was excited about meeting up with her, but not enough to go the extra mile.

I wrestled with questions and answers. I was troubled for days because I blamed myself for not moving fast enough. I thought to myself,

"What if God allowed her to call me so I could comfort her?"

"What if He had moved her to contact me so I could say a word to make a difference in her life?"

"What if the time she called was the moment for me to lead her to the Lord?" "What if she needed money or something and could only trust me with filling that need?"

"What if... What if...? What if...?"

The funeral brought a lot of our classmates out of the "woodwork:" those who teased and poked at us; those who we thought would have made it to the "big times," but hadn't; those who wanted to be friends with us, but did not want to risk wearing the badge of dishonor as we did; and those who cared like I did.

Of all the classmates and friends that gathered, I was the only one that was asked to speak at her funeral. What a great opportunity! What an honor! But as much as one may think so, I was afraid and guilty. Here was my chance to make it up to Calista. Now was the time to wake others up to the reality of life—it's short! This was my only chance to say something that I never made the time to say.

Although not a poet, I wrote a poem chronicling our friendship from the time of middle school to college. As I read the poem, occasional chuckles, moans of agreement, and random sniffs, as if popcorn was slowly popping, could be heard from the audience.

Calista could not hear all the things I had to say about her and our childhood, neither could she hear that I was sorry that I did not make the time to meet up with her. I spoke of how precious life is and how important it is to cherish the time God has given all of us.

"Stop being so busy making a life for you," I said. "Rest and reflect on your greatest asset—this moment, this time. Make the most of it with the people God has entrusted to you—family, friends, and strangers." I struggled to get the words out, but I knew someone in the audience needed to hear them. Hear them? They did. Acted upon them? I didn't know if anyone would. But, *will you?*

REFLECTION ON LESSONS LEARNED

←*←*←*←*←*←*←

I lost the opportunity to witness to or be a source of possible cheer to a friend. The months rolled by and before long they became years. There was no preoccupation with getting in touch with or meeting up with her. I had moved on with my educational career and she had too. But somehow, I am left with the thought, "Leave a little of God with everyone you meet." Paul, in 2 Timothy 4:1-8, encourages us to proclaim the good news of Jesus Christ. We ought to be consistent with it too. *"Be instant in season and out of season."*

Look, the conditions may not always be favorable, but you have to do it. You may have to do it when it seems that it's the most inopportune time. But the time is what we construe it to be. It more than likely *is* the time the person needs it most. I've done it, as scared as I was. And I've walked away saying, "Whew! Boy. That was a close one."

Experience is the greatest teacher. You don't have to wait for something terrible to happen before you realize that the window of opportunity is closed. Glean from the nuggets I've provided to help you along the way:

- Don't let an opportunity go by. It might be that person's last time walking this path.
- Send a "Thinking of you" card to a friend you've not heard from in a long time.
- Give a hug to that elderly lady that sits near the middle aisle of your church.
- Visit a hospital with long stemmed roses and randomly pass each one out to patients and/or their relatives.
- Tell a friend how much you love and appreciate them.
- Read a book to a sick or elderly person.

- Call that brother or sister you've not spoken to in years (for whatever reason) and let them know you're sorry.
- Visit a homeless shelter and/or senior citizen home and spread some laughter and cheer.
- Invite a neighbor over for tea.
- Tell a child you are proud of him/her.
- Pray for God to lead you to the right person EVERY day and give a word of comfort and cheer.
- Have a smile and a good word for everyone you meet.

The list could be longer and I know you probably came up with some good ones as you were reading mine. But make it an everyday practice to make the most of the time God has given you. Your words, your acts of kindness, your thought of love will almost certainly make a difference in the life of someone.

Don't create a record of "lost opportunities."

CHAPTER THREE

DOUBLE FOR YOUR TROUBLE

*"What lies behind us and what lies before us are small
matters compared to what lies within us."*
—Ralph Waldo Emerson

N ow "right off the bat" I truly want you to know that I do
not claim to know everything. But I do know trouble
when I see it. Not only do I recognize it, but I also know
when it's closing in on me.

I attended the University of the District of Columbia
for four years and enjoyed the college life. I did quite well
academically and was encouraged by professors and friends
to go for a law degree. I come from a family where all the children wanted to take up professions that commanded respect
and a great salary—Engineer, Accountant, Veterinarian, and
Lawyer—but would not require all of our youthful years in
school. My mind was made up. My heart was fixed. I was
going to be the first attorney in the family.

Applying to law school was not a problem for me as I
had the grades and the extracurricular activities to show for
it, but I had a nemesis—standardized testing—and it seemed
a formidable task for me. It seemed to be the only stumbling
block to fulfilling my dream.

My Dad and I decided we would do all we could to help me prepare for the law school admission test. We informed no one of my decision to continue to graduate school because I feared the outcome—a rejection letter. I took the examination and received two extra points over what was required for my socio-economic background: black, female, and lower middle class. I was excited, but something began to stir in my spirit. Before I could get my scores and applications to the prospective schools, I began to wrestle with the question, "Is this the path you want me to take, Lord?"

What great timing! "Why didn't I ask this question before I spent my father's hard-earned money preparing and sitting for the exam," I asked myself? I knew the answer to that question—prestige. Yes, prestige awaited me so I quickly won that battle and resumed sending off my applications. Harvard was my first choice, but I knew my parents couldn't afford it. Georgetown was next on my list; I knew I wouldn't have a problem getting in there. I decided to wait for a response from them before I contacted any other schools. Little did I know, God had other plans.

Waiting for the responses, I decided to fast and seek God's direction. Yep, you got it correct. I did it after the fact. But from where I stood, I knew God to be all-powerful and capable of changing the hands of time in my favor whether I consulted Him before or after. Yeah, right.

Well, while seeking Him, God took my attention to the scripture in Habakkuk 2:3, *"But these things I plan won't happen right away. Slowly, steadily, surely, the time approaches when the vision will be fulfilled. If it seems slow, do not despair, for these things will surely come to pass. Just be patient! They will not be overdue a single day!"* (LB).

All right, what did He go do that for? I mean I have my plans, my aspirations, my path set for success. What did He mean by, "...these thing won't happen right away...?" Why did He have to mention "slowly"? I've got things to do, places to go, and lots of money to make. Time waits for no man, and I surely was not about to wait for time. Come to think of it, I thought that my plans were His plans and He would be glad for me. I would be one of the greatest Christian corporate lawyers if there ever was one. Not good English there, but that's the way I felt and that's how I was communing with God.

Needless to say, He won. I received one of those thin white envelopes that in essence said, "Don't even try it. Look elsewhere!" After reading it, tears filled my eyes. I struggled to lift the water-drenched lids and focused my attention upward. Yes, I knew I couldn't call anyone else to console me. I knew I couldn't dare try and have anyone else answer my list of questions. So, yes, I managed to look toward heaven, peering pass my fuchsia painted ceiling, through the aged wooden floorboards of the attic floor, through the insulated paneling that lined the attic ceiling, pass the 70-year-old slated roof and said, "Why?"

"Why was I denied such an awesome opportunity? I've been a good girl. I pay my tithes. I'm obedient to my folks. I treat people right—most of the time. I proved that I can do well in school... I... I... I..." Above all the narcissistic responses I blurted out, I heard a caring, gentle voice break through the barriers of time, pass the agony and whimper of my heart, that whispered, "You cannot at this time My purpose see, but all is well that's done by Me."

Okay, yes, I was hurting and I was possibly too dependent on hearing something to bring solace to this urgent disappointing feeling, but what was that that I had heard? Words of such magnitude did not readily heal the wounds of rejection that seemed to permeate my entire twenty-three year old body. I sat on the bed awhile pondering, musing, and checking my attitude. Not long after, I took a deep breath, got up from my slumped position, walked over to the chest of drawers, placed the letter back into the envelope, and tucked it away into my "special" drawer.

I stood there, hoping something miraculous would happen in my favor, and sighed as if in resignation, "Okay, Lord. I'm yours, what do you want me to do now?"

Now there were some around me who thought that I was wasting the precious brain God gave me by not pursuing my dreams. I did not jump at the opportunity to let them know that God had had other plans in mind for me.

To keep some people at bay and money in my pocket, I applied for a job that required use of my Political Science and English background. Working as an assistant to the editor for a non-profit police organization newspaper was not something I envisioned myself doing for the rest of my life. I wanted something that somehow hinted to the life I dreamed about since elementary school. I worked at the organization for only a few months before the Lord led me to a Trak Auto store to get mud flaps for my 1979 used BMW. It was my pride and joy; my only ticket to show that I was heading for the rich life.

To make a very long story short, I met a lady in the store who recommended that I apply for a researcher position at an investigative firm. I took her up on the offer and was hired without prior experience. They later told me they took a chance with me because they loved my personality. "Your personality is great for the field," one said. Basically, I did not look like a private investigator (the term "researcher" is used outside the office). Therefore, I almost became a master of pre-texting, or getting information out of people without them knowing neither who I was nor whom I represented.

I worked for this international investigative firm for exactly seven years. I say the word "exactly" because the month I was hired was the same month I was fired. Did I just say fired? Yes, I did. What an ugly word!

Well, in my sixth year, things began to look very bleak for me at this firm. I went from being the "sunshine" of the office to the "ridiculed one" on the investigative staff. I can't go into details as to what exactly happened due to confidential papers signed by both parties at the settlement agreement meeting, but I will say this, I was the only African-American investigator at the headquarter office, and God blessed me to leave there with my head up with honor and integrity. Yeah!

As I was saying before...my sixth year began with a downward spiral. I realized that things were not as peachy as they seemed. I began to seek God for direction. He told me to stay at the firm and do not quit while in the "fire." Did I hear Him? You would think so, but my actions proved contrary.

I began to send out resumes to as many firms, organizations, and agencies as I could; however, each of them responded with the same comment, "You are over-qualified for the position..." Some even offered me the position with a pay cut, but I was not about to go backwards. No way, not at this juncture of the game.

Things became almost unbearable for me at the firm. God was right. I was placed in the middle of the fire. Each morning I woke up, I felt the dread of meeting the fake smiles, and the empty talks my colleagues would try to have with me. I knew I had become the enemy, the subject of water fountain talks. I knew that the board meetings that excluded me meant that trouble was on its way with a vengeance. But what could I do about it? The only outlet I had was prayer. I began to enter into my prayer closet at work—my office— more often than I had before; I would often rush home just to lay it all out at Jesus' feet.

I sought the Lord for covering every day, and prayed for the very ones I knew did not wish me well. Was it easy? Initially no, but I learned that the more I prayed for them, the more sympathy and care God placed in my heart towards them. I began to also see the path that God had destined for my life. But, it required more than just knowing it. It called for confession and repentance.

When I took the job, I was still of the mindset that I was going to build a fortune for myself through the legal profession. This line of work seemed close enough to the real thing—being a lawyer. But guess what? I now had to confess my selfish desires to the Lord and repent for wanting to build my own empire and not acknowledge Him in all my ways.

I now realized that the path God was leading me toward had nothing to do with me. When I stripped away all the titles, the degrees, the accomplishments, the awards, accolades, and somewhat rich associates, I saw that it was all vanity just like the wise man Solomon exclaimed in the book of Ecclesiastes. A dear neighbor of mine, Louie, once said to me, "Don't walk by life. Stop along the way and enjoy the things of value—the birds, a flower, a smile from an older couple walking together hand-in-hand..."

My road to success did not allot for any of that stuff. I wanted to be rich and self-sufficient at a very young age. I was not going to work the majority of my life, as my parents, and not get a chance to enjoy it in my somewhat youthful years. Time moves, and I was trying to keep instep with father time. But then I found out something riveting... life goes on whether I am here or not.

What was the rush? Where was I going so fast? I found out life was no longer about me. I found myself asking, "What is it that You want me to do, God?"

Don't you think sometimes that God is funny? I mean the Man (no disrespect intended) has such a sense of humor. He'll let you have your way for a time, let you have your say so, your stint with fame, riches, and glory. And then with a gentle blow from His lips, shake up everything in your world and snap you back to reality. It's almost as if you can feel the earth move under your feet to the point where you say, "Okay, God! You talking to me?"

Now all along He has been talking, but we're just too busy making plans for ourselves and planting our roots deeper in this earthly soil to the point of not hearing Him. What about, *"[Laying] up for yourselves treasures in heaven, where neither moth nor rust doth corrupt, and where thieves do not break through nor steal [?]"* (Matthew 6:20).

Well, I know. It's not easy to lay up stuff you can't see with your physical eyes, nor touch with your hands. But let me tell you this. The treasures that I've learned to store up in the presence of God are far more expensive than the ones earth has to offer. And I mean to tell you that it was acquired through hurt, pain, disappointment, and loneliness. I worked hard for "them" treasures!

The opening of my seventh year at the firm was no different from the sixth one. I was awakened one morning early with the words,

"Double for your trouble."

"Ok, God," I said when I heard the words, "that's a great theme for the upcoming youth service."

I was the church interim youth president at the time and within months our highly celebrated service would be here. As the day traveled on, I tried to remember the words I had heard earlier that morning. Tried as I did, I could not for the life of me remember a word.

I was threatened at work that day and decided to pack up and leave. The Lord reminded me that I was not to quit, but to let them fire me. I struggled with the ridicule, the back stabbings, the willful orchestrated lies, and the cunning approaches. "But how long was I to endure this?" I asked. I was not necessarily addressing the question to the Lord; I just wanted to get it out of my system. I rationalized as much as I could, but no resolution was at hand.

Bishop T.D. Jakes† was in town for a couple days at Great Mount Calvary Holy Church, Washington, D.C., and a few of my friends encouraged me to attend the service. I went the first night and enjoyed the sermon, but I was too caught up in what was happening to allow the words to minister fully to my spirit. I'm sure something passed its way through the thickness of my distress and sat dormant, waiting for the right timing. But I, in the depths of my pain, could not readily embrace and enjoy the powerful words that flowed from his lips to my ears.

When my friends dropped me off that night, they begged me to come with them the next day. I came up with every excuse in the book—

"I gotta get my hair done for the weekend. I have to prepare for the Sabbath. I don't know what I'm wearing to church and I may have to wash clothes. I..."

The list went on. Would they buy it? No. I was threatened to be there or suffer the consequences. Lisa, I can still hear you now loud and clear in my ears,

"You betta be there or else!"

I attended the service that Friday night and went through the motions during the praise and worship session. When they announced the entrance of T.D. Jakes, I stood and applauded. The applause was not out of recognition. Rather, I was imitating what everyone else was doing. I didn't even hear them call his name. I had many thoughts accompanied by varied emotional pain as a result of the attack I received that day. So everything around me was happening without my being aware of it consciously.

The man of God came on the platform and began to worship the Lord. The crowd stood and praised the Lord with cheers and hands flailing in the air. I stood too, but it was not to worship, rather, it was to see Bishop Jakes above the heads of the people in front of me.

He began His sermon with the congregation reading the scripture. I couldn't tell you what it was because it just did not move me. He began to expound on the Word and to break it down only the way he can. I listened, but not intently. Then suddenly, it was if I was alone in the audience with just Bishop T.D. Jakes. It seemed as if a spotlight had engulfed my being; I became enthralled by the silence and then the sound of his voice. The jolt my spirit needed was about to spring forth with intended results as Bishop Jakes uttered the words,

"God is going to give you *double for your trouble.*"

All the noise around me ceased. It felt like the words grabbed at every fiber of my being. I gave out a scream that could have awakened Goliath. I grabbed Lisa's hand and said,

"That's what the Lord said to me this morning! That's what He said… 'Double for your trouble.' "

I began to jump up and down with tears running down my face. I cried. I cried. I cried. And I cried. I cried so hard that I believe the person sitting in front of me had to move. It did not matter who was near. I began bending over the chair and screaming inside myself. As I bent over the chair crying, mucous began hanging from my nose, and my face felt like it was about to explode. It didn't matter to me what I looked like at that moment. Something supernatural was happening.

I hung onto the words of Bishop Jakes as if they were a life jacket thrown from a ship anchored in the deepest waters. I knew what God had said that morning, but could not for the life of me remember it all day long. Those words meant so much to me. They seemed like the guidepost I needed to stay on the path, however painful.

Bishop Jakes said it! In those few seconds, I saw how it applied to my current situation. I realized that God was dealing with me for something greater. As I wept and cried out to the Lord, I sorrowfully said,

"Lord, give me back the wasted years so I can start all over again."

Immediately after I said it, Bishop Jakes exclaimed,

"And God is giving you back the wasted years..."

Okay, by now I was losing my mind with crying and rocking back and forth in a fetal position over the chair. Now I know what those prayer warriors were talking about at tarrying service. The tears were flowing and the mucous had no shame. This is the stuff I needed when I was twelve.

I continued to travail before the Lord. I cried, I howled, I screamed, I prayed. I cried, I howled, I screamed, I prayed.

Trying to gain some level of composure and decency, I began lifting myself from the fetal position and prayed,

"Oh, God, take away the spirit of depression from me now."

Before the period could be attached to the sentence, I heard Bishop Jakes say,

"And God is lifting that spirit of depression from off you, now."

That was it! I was no longer any good. In the Spirit, I saw a huge black blanket lift off my shoulders and head, then, it was carried out of the building. I cried, screamed, and moaned even louder.

I had no voice left to scream. I grabbed my torso and moaned as the tears rolled down my face. Anyone looking on would think that I was in excruciating pain. But it was not pain that brought me to this position. It was a moan of "God you remembered me... You see me."

Did I care if anyone was watching me? Did I take note of my appearance? Was I concerned with what my friends thought at the time? Of course not! I had crossed over a dark, hopeless, and self-destructive chasm. I got the release I needed to continue on the journey. I received the healing for my inner soul. I was encouraged that the Lord had taken note of me.

I've always wanted to write Bishop Jakes to let him know how God used him mightily to save someone from drowning in sorrow and possible suicide. But I thought he would not get my letter as he probably receives hundreds like mine. I do hope he gets to read this book as a testimony to his ministry.

Needless to say, that was such a refreshing experience for me that I felt I could handle anything that came my way after that. And came it did. I was fired a few months after that experience. It was not until then that I began to really experience my "double for your trouble."

I went from making over 30,000 dollars a year with bonuses and perks, to living off less than 5,000 dollars a year for the next two years. Now my salary may not sound like a lot of money today, but it was 1997, and I had no major bills. To me, I was living large.

God brought many changes in my life that I did not expect. With the changes came pain, reproach, lies, heartstring hurts, and much more. God basically said, "Look, Hewlette, enough is enough! You have work to do for me. I have great plans for you and in order to help you reach them, I must shake everything in your life. Anything that has true foundation will remain, but every thing else that has taken my place must go."

Did the Lord speak loud and clear? Yes, He did. Some of the friendships I had acquired over the years and thought would never be shaken were either toppled or shifted. The financial kingdom I was building for myself was nowhere to be found. My good name was run through the mud, and I became the subject of conversations at dinner tables, one-day church trips, overnight gatherings, and parties.

I remember overhearing, in the Spirit, one such conversation a particular family was having regarding me. I vowed to come to church and berate them for it, but I knew that was not the reason why God had allowed me to hear them in the Spirit. God was teaching me how to show love even when I knew the opposite was being shown to me. He was also showing me that restraint is far better than an uncontrolled tongue. But more importantly, He was perfecting a gift He had placed within me. Scared as I was when I realized this, I knew His call upon my life was not ordinary.

Losing my job was one thing, but losing my brand new Toyota Camry was totally out of the question. I remember when the Lord told me to stay at my job until they fired me. I was scared and doubted if He would take care of my needs. The entire time the enemy plagued me with the thought of the "repo man" coming to get my vehicle while I slept.

My car note was $425 per month. I had no problems making the payments while I was employed, but time had passed and my savings were affected by it. Not having anything coming in began to weigh heavily on me. I only had a few hundred bucks left from my savings to make about three more payments and pay my other bills.

The day finally came where all I had was $400 dollars left in my bank account. There was nothing in the checking and the savings account was about to do a disappearing act. Now let me tell you, I am not, nor ever have been one to practice writing bounced checks. It's not the godly thing to do. But, here I was at my Red Sea with no Moses and no rod. Yes, I see the mountain of debts on each side, the soon to be empty bank account in front of me, and the "repo man" closing in fast behind. But what did God promise me?

I searched for His promises in the crowded and scared corners of my mind. I wished for them to make sense to me in this time of what seemed to be great embarrassment. Maybe it doesn't seem that way to you, but it did to me. Yes me, Hewlette, the one who always had money to give to other people; the one who bought things for others; the one who surprised friends on their birthday with something from their wish list. Yes, I was down on hard times, and hard times did not make its bed fluffy and soft for me either. It was down right hard!

So there I was, trying to hold on to the promises of God and facing reality. Now I knew that David in Psalm 37:25 said, *"I have been young, and now am old; yet have I not seen the righteous forsaken, nor His seed begging bread..."* But how and through whom was my "bread" coming.

I began to check myself to see if I fell into that category — you know, "the righteous." Well, I felt I did and decided to trust God for a miracle. I also thought of Hebrews 11:1, which states, *"Now faith is the substance of things hoped for, the evident of things not seen."* But I knew I didn't have all of the money, and I didn't know anyone who could readily loan it to me. So, I closed my eyes and hoped it would appear. I believed it would come, but I wrestled with the thought of it not showing up in time to pay the full amount.

As I sat there with the envelope sealed and ready for mailing, I said, "God, I wrote this check for the full amount. I am asking you to put the extra twenty-five dollars on it for me." I did not care how God was going to do it. I needed a miracle badly and had nowhere else to turn. The friends who could possible help had walked away. The doors that would normally be open appeared to be one push away from being slammed right into my face. And my pride would not let me beg my parents for twenty-five dollars.

I was alone now. The only place I could look was up. I began to expect something unusual to happen. Where did this feeling suddenly come from? I did not know at the time, but I began to expect it to be all right. I remembered God is always in control.

I got up to mail the payment and heard my telephone ringing. It was a good friend of mine from the investigative firm. She said,

"Hewlette, I've been thinking a lot about you and wondered if you would like to have lunch with me today?"

I abruptly responded with a resounding,

"Yes! Where would you like to meet?"

It was a welcomed call, as I was growing weary of being at home and doing chores everyday. I finally got a chance to go somewhere.

We met at our favorite sushi restaurant, Café Asia, and reminisced about the good old days at the firm. As the time of our meal came to a close, she squeezed my hand and placed a card in front of me.

"This is for you to let you know I miss you and hope everything is working out for you," she said.

I reassured her every thing was going good in graduate school and that I was trusting God for everything now. Oops, I forgot to tell you. I applied and was accepted to Johns Hopkins School of Business and Education. I began taking classes six months before I was fired. Okay, back to the story...

I thanked her for the card and resumed eating my sushi.

"Please Hewlette, open the card now," she begged.

I wondered why she was in such a rush for me to open the card. It's a greeting card. I've seen them before in many shapes, sizes, and colors. What is so different about this one besides the possible mushy words on the inside?

I put down my chopsticks, dabbed the sides of my mouth with the napkin, paused, and looked at her.

"Hurry up, Hewlette. Open it... Come on!" she urged.

Making it humorously agonizing as possible for her, I slowly slid my forefinger under the edge of the envelope's flap and ripped open the carefully sealed white pouch. What an amazing miracle! What a carefully divine timing!

I don't even remember reading the card slow enough for the words to make sense to me at the time. All I saw was a check for twenty-five dollars. Yes! Here it was. My expected end! Another chance to keep the "repo man" at bay! An answer to a promise!

My friend probably got the biggest bear hug in her life, for I held on to her and started praising God in her ear.

"I hope you don't mind, but I'm leaving now to deposit this in the bank," I exclaimed.

She smiled as I explained to her the miracle God wrought through her. Did she understand what took place? Maybe, but the magnitude of it could only be truly understood by one who finds him/herself in that position.

Is He an on-time God? Yes indeed He is! That was an awesome and gracious move of God on my behalf. While I was at home wrestling with my faith, God was orchestrating the answer on my former job.

Yes, the trouble had begun, but my double would not be very far behind, or would it? No thing, person, or situation can deter me from walking into that precious promise. Only time would tell just how faithful I would be.

Yes, that twenty-five dollar blessing was on time. Now that I think about it, maybe if I had asked the Lord for more the check would have been larger. Hallelujah!!

REFLECTION ON LESSONS LEARNED

←*←*←*←*←*←*←

There are so many things that God has designed for us. If He were to show them to us all at once, we would possibly doubt if they were all earmarked for us and probably question if it were possible. But He is so gracious that He prepares us to meet each challenge so that we can embrace these wonderful things in confidence and gratitude.

There are several lessons I learned from the experiences in this chapter. I did not list them all here because the list would encroach on the pages of the other chapters. But, I hope you can glean from what follows:

- The things we acquire in this life can never transfer for credit in the kingdom of God. As a matter of fact, it pales in comparison to the glory that will be revealed in us.
- The degrees, prestige, "good" name, and social status we crave are not the pre-requisites needed to gain an audience with Jesus Christ. They are not what give us value. It is the mark of His hand upon our lives.
- As much as I pushed to get what I planned to get out of life, I came to an awesome awakening—only the works I do for Christ will follow me into the kingdom. The path that I had chosen proved that I would not have the procession that was required to enter the presence of the King on that great day.

Money! Money! Money! The world "turns" on money. King Solomon said that it answers all things. I guess he meant those things that call its name. But the truth of the matter is that we depend on money to acquire the "best" things in life. And therefore, those of us who were not born into wealth know that the only way to legally acquire this elusive recycled paper is to work for it. Work hard and long. We then begin to look to our jobs as our means of support. But guess what I learned?

- I realized that my job was a resource God provided to meet my needs at the time. Resources change, but my Source never does. God remained faithful and constant throughout my whole ordeal.
- Never box God in. Allow Him to surprise you.
- God sends friends in your life for a reason, a season, and for a lifetime. Cherish each stage and learn as much as you can where you are and with what you have. It's okay to move on; it's even more special when a friendship shifts or closes on good terms.

Pastor John Hagee had John Maxwell as a guest speaker in one of his services. Maxwell said that the following statement is the platform for a miracle, "When there is a need sensed by a few and each individual understands his responsibility and gives his all regardless of the cost, then a miracle will take place."

The money I needed to pay my car note came when I trusted God, wrote a check (at the chance of paying more in the long run for bouncing it), and stretched out on His promises. I had nothing to lose but a car. I was not going to lose my faith, not my newfound relationship, not my anointing, and not my name (the one He gave me) that is written in the Lamb's book of life. With that in mind, the ground was set for a miracle.

What is the reason for a test? What exactly does God want from me when I go through hardships, disappointments, betrayal, and pain? Well, I found out early in the game. One day when I was meditating, the Holy Spirit led me to Isaiah 48:10: *"Behold, I have refined thee, but not with silver; I have chosen thee in the furnace of affliction."*

- I was being chosen for something special. I was being equipped with tools that would later be of benefit to the kingdom of God and to me. God was hammering some bad stuff out of me, so I could embrace the gifts He had ordained for my life before the world was created.

- It was God's way of letting me know that this was not an accident. This whole "Double for your trouble" was a set up for something monumental—a push to the next dimension in my relationship with Him.

- Although the struggle was tough, the person He molded and fashioned in adversity was now able to give Him "true worship" that's birthed out of my experiences with Him, rather than what I have read about Him. I am now becoming a living, walking, breathing oracle of praise.

Isaiah 61:6-7 encourages us by saying, *"You will be called Priests of the Lord, Ministers of our God; you will be fed with the treasures of the nations and will boast in their riches. For your shame ye shall have double; …you will inherit a double portion of prosperity and everlasting joy."*

What an awesome promise. Imagine if someone said to you, "You're going to be laughed at, talked about, rejected, broke, disgusted, and heartbroken, BUT it's just for a short while. I'll give you double for what you lose, and no matter what happens from here, you will always be joyful."

Crazy? Not really, because sometimes we go through things and do not take the time to see if it is divinely planned. God doesn't just let stuff happen to us. No! He wants to maximize every experience we go through. He's a God of blessings and He wants us to walk fully into it without any hindrances.

This scripture means a lot to me because part of it is the promise I received, "Double for your trouble." I've already begun to see the manifestation of the blessings that accompany the promise. You'll get to read about some of it in the chapter entitled, *"Just Enough Light for the Journey."*

I received these and more not because I was perfect, good, or always obedient, not at all. But, they came because of His promises to me and my faithfulness in the time of great pain. He knows the intent of my heart, so even when I struggle to keep my head above water—He is there to throw me a life jacket and help me ashore so I can rest.

Your "Double for your trouble" may be around the corner. But I encourage you to embrace it and watch the awesome move of God in your life. His love for you is worth it!

CHAPTER FOUR

THE ENEMY WITHIN

"Whatever does not destroy me makes me stronger."
—Nietzsche

When my feet gave way to the sheet of ice that paved the way to my car that early February morning, I unconsciously protected my fresh hair-do while going down without advanced notice. I landed flat on my back, but managed to protect the "do." With face against the sky, I laid there for a couple seconds trying to figure out what had just happened.

June, a good friend of mine, came running out the house to help this disheveled soul to her feet. As she ventured to raise me up, I reached out to stop her 'cause I knew the "Captain Kirk" boots I was wearing would land me in the same position again.

"Let me roll over to my knees then help me up," I said.

With some obvious difficulty, we both labored together to get me to my feet. What a sight that was. So glad it was still dark outside.

I drove to work that day praying and wishing nothing would come of the fall I experienced. Yes, it would have been a good, legitimate reason to stay home from work that day, but I loved my job and the students I taught. Seriously, I'm not kidding you. Thank the Lord! I went through the day without any pain. As a matter of fact, I did not remember that I had fallen.

Later, during that week, we were told that there was a snowstorm headed our way, but not as ferocious as the one we had just three weeks prior. The city prepared itself for the worst. I got up extra early that Wednesday morning to beat the mad rush hour traffic. But when I listened to the news, we had a two-hour delay due to the snow. I made it to work later than the time permitted and was just thawing out when the announcement came that school would be closing within the next thirty minutes.

Okay, I don't use profanity and neither do I swear. But, if there were anyone close to me that day, I probably would have told that person to do so on my behalf. Here I was—wet, cold, and irritated from arguing with people—unbeknownst to them of course—who claimed the State said they were qualified to drive. That's right, just because a person has his or her license does not confirm that he or she knows how to drive, especially in the snow. Furthermore, I was not about to go back out there and sit in traffic for three to four hours trying to get back home.

Pat, affectionately known as my "Caucasian mother" and a wonderful colleague, extended the offer to stay at her house until the weather got better. I accepted, as this was a home I was accustomed to frequenting, especially for house-sitting duties. The weather became worse; school officials announced that school would be closed on the morrow. It was good news for me, especially since I was studying for my certification exams.

On the following day at around 4:00 p.m., I felt an unusual pain shoot through the walls of my stomach. I leaned against the closest furniture in Pat's house to stabilize my weight on my legs. I called out to Pat,

"I don't feel so good. I have a sharp pain in my stomach."

"Well, why don't you try going to the bathroom to see if it would help any," she suggested.

I hobbled to the bathroom like a 9-month pregnant woman. I wrestled with the pain to pull my pants down, but even that created more drama than was necessary. I sat on the toilet hoping something would happen to relieve the excruciating pain that engulfed my body. I broke out in a cold sweat. Then came the heavy breathing as a woman who is about to deliver a baby.

My breathing got progressively heavier, and between each breath I whispered,

"Jesus, Jesus, Jesus! Move the pain, Lord. Move the pain, please."

It felt like the pain was moving from my chest, to my stomach, then to my pelvic area, then to my legs.

"Yes, Lord. Move it. Move. Move it. It's coming down, Lord. Yes, keep moving it... Move it down to my legs and straight out my feet, Lord," I said.

I started thanking the Lord for moving the pain right down my legs and out of my body, but my praise was interrupted by a knock at the door.

"Are you okay in there?"

I didn't answer 'cause I couldn't answer. The pain had gripped me so intensely that all I could take were small breaths.

"Hewlette, is everything alright?" Pat said with a concerned voice.

With every ounce of energy that I could muster, I painstakingly said, "Y-e-s."

"You want me to make you some tea," she asked?

I could not get a word out. To allay her fears I grumbled something that sounded like a "no."

"Okay, let me know if you need anything," she said.

I rolled off the toilet seat to the floor, pulled my pants halfway up my buttocks, crawled over to the door, and with the last bit of strength I had, pushed open the bathroom door. Unable to talk or scream for help, I began banging on the wall for Pat's attention.

"Oh my God, what's happened to you?"

I heard her, but I couldn't respond. I lay there with my mouth ajar, drooling as if I did not have my wits about me. She ran for the cordless phone and called 911. I could hear her trying to explain to them what was going on with me, but she was having some trouble, and I could not help her. She sat there on the floor with me—I was in the fetal position with part of my head and torso in her lap; my legs and feet were cropped in between the wall and her.

Pat began to rock me back and forth to soothe my hurt, but unbeknownst to her it created a whirlwind of more pain; yet, I could not communicate it to her. I tried by squeezing her hand, but I think she thought I was doing so in order to brace for the pain. The paramedics came and tried to talk to me, but I just could not talk because of the intensity of the pain. One of the paramedics told me to squeeze his hand twice for "yes" and once for "no" as he asked me several questions. They tried to get me to stand up, but the pain intensified; I buckled beneath its bite.

"Aaaaaaaaahhh!" I screamed as the paramedic picked me up in the fetal position, placed me on the gurney, and stretched my body out as best he could. As soon as my face hit the cold winter air, everything that I had eaten that day came flying out of my mouth like a motion picture horror flick. I consider myself a very strong woman, one who can hold up under stress and immense pain, but nothing in the past could hold a torch up to what I was experiencing that night. By the time we reached the hospital, I was ready and waiting for the Lord to call me home.

It was not until three o'clock the next morning, after I gain full consciousness, that I was informed I had experienced the trauma of a ruptured ovarian cist. They decided to keep me a few days for observation for the cist and for something very unusual they detected while conducting tests on me during the night. On Saturday morning, I had a visit from a doctor I had never seen in my life. There is a reason why I say it like that. It will become clearer later. Well anyway, he came into my room sat at the foot of my bed and said,

"Do you know you have a tumor in your abdomen?"

"Yes, Sir," I responded.

"Well, it needs to come out now 'cause it's pressing against your intestine and stomach. Soon it will have severe impact on your spine," he informed me.

"Doctor, I know it's there. It's been there for a couple years now, but all the doctors I've been to want to give me a total hysterectomy," I responded.

"Well, Ms. Pearson, this thing has got to go or it'll impede your organs and bring damage, possibly death," he cautioned.

I didn't have an answer to give him because I had been told that a couple times before. But, I had been waiting on the Lord to heal me for many years. I could have been free from this thing many years ago, but I told the Lord that if He were not going to heal me, I would die with it.

Sounds stupid, idiotic, insane, and foolish doesn't it? Well, that's where my faith was, and I was not going to sway from it no matter how much pain I encountered, or how large the tumor grew. It wasn't cancerous; at least not since the last time the doctor checked it.

Many people did not know I had a tumor in my abdomen. I wore my clothes in such a way that took the emphasis off my stomach. It was not that it protruded severely to the point of obvious sight, but I knew that my stomach area had gotten larger, and my belly had begun to lap over my waistline.

Playing with my nieces and nephews is something I enjoy doing. But there were times they would run up into me and land right in the spot of the tumor. I would have to say, "Can't play with Auntie Hewie like that, guys." Sometimes they would run to greet me and their shoulders or heads would rest right in the area, but I had to grin and bear the pain so as to not ruin their affectionate greetings.

Having the pleasure of sleeping on my stomach was something I had not had the opportunity to do in over nine to ten years. If I ventured to do so, the tumor seemed like it would stand up like a baby and make my sleep so uncomfortable. And forget bending over and tying my shoelace. That was a no, no. If I tried to do it, the pain associated with the pressure on my pelvic area would send me flying to the bed to curl up and wish the excruciating pain away.

Necessity being the mother of invention, I had to come up with a way of tying my shoes without aggravating this thing. Thank God for stairs. That's how I solved the problem. I would go down a few flights of stairs, turn back around, lift my leg up on the steps in front of me, and tie my shoes. The same went for buckling and putting on my shoes—the difficult ones at least.

Great, pulsating, shooting, ice pick pain was associated with this tumor. There were times I was engaged in conversation and out of the blue, a pain would hit me so much that it would cause me to react to the dismay of the person to whom I was speaking. It also had emotional ills that accompanied its presence. One minute you could be happy and content, the next you would be fighting the pangs of depression and melancholy or simply be upset for no reason. Yes, mood swings would overcome me at times.

This thing was no joke! It affected every aspect of my life: emotional, physical, and spiritual. You're probably wondering how it affected me spiritually. I guess I would wonder the same thing too, but seeing I had the experience, let me explain it to you.

I had been in ministry for several years. I had prayed for people and they received healing. I'd spoken prophetic words over the lives of individuals, and some had even contacted me and told me the words of the Lord came to pass. I had given words of knowledge and had encouraged many. But when it came time for me to get my healing, to receive my deliverance, and to be set free from this thing, nothing happened.

Now you tell me! Wouldn't that affect you spiritually? Wouldn't it cause you to question your walk with the Lord? Wouldn't you question God and ask, "When is my turn?"

Look, I preached with this thing, taught with it, prayed for others with it, witnessed about God's goodness with it, and made people laugh with it. But, when bedtime came and I ventured to sleep on my stomach, it would remind me that it was there. In the night, I would feel it pulsating and sometimes moving. It truly acted as if it were a fetus growing into a baby.

Don't think that I ever charged God, or was angry at Him about it. No! I held onto faith the entire time, but I was also looking at both sides of life and realizing that things just weren't adding up fairly.

The doctor sat there waiting for me to give him an answer. I told him I would let him know by the afternoon. He left the room, and I turned my face to the wall and cried. I said,

"Lord, do you want me to do this. I need you to heal me. I don't want a hysterectomy."

I cried and sat up in bed for a while. As I began to drift off to sleep, I heard a soft gentle voice say,

"Go ahead, take the operation. I am with you."

I breathed a small sigh of relief and slipped into sleep.

"Ms. Pearson, Ms. Pearson!" broke the calm slumber. I answered with a foreboding tone,

"Yes?"

It was the doctor coming back to check on my decision. That's right, I said, "check." Assessing his countenance from the last visit, I believed he thought I was still under the influence of the medication given to me earlier and not able to understand the ramifications of not acting on this thing right away.

"Yes, I'll go ahead and have the surgery," I said.

"Good. I've planned it for late Monday morning around 11 o'clock," he informed me.

"Gosh, that was quick," I thought.

"Why couldn't it be Tuesday or Wednesday," I muttered.

Of course what I wanted at this time did not matter. My staying alive was now the focal point of everything I would have to say or do.

By this time, flowers and cards from well-wishers were pouring in. Friends and family gathered at my bedside to wish me well. My brother, Aldean, spared no time in commenting that the only thing that was missing in my room was an organ. He said that I had so many flowers that my room resembled a funeral home. Everyone responded with a hearty chuckle, but I was too caught up in the fact that I was possibly going to lose my uterus because of this wicked unwanted thing.

A very strong, unannounced pain hit my abdomen on Sunday afternoon causing the doctor to prescribe a knockout pain-killing drug—Percocet. I slept while the drug took effect, but as soon as its powers wore off, I was back to writhing in excruciating pain. What was causing it? The doctors did not know and I really didn't care at the time. I just wanted to be rid of this ghastly painful feeling that permeated my entire body.

The pain intensified that Sunday night as June sat at the side of my bed and held my hands to bring comfort. I remember asking her to get the Bible and read Psalm 81. While rocking back and forth in pain, I heard a voice say, "Read Psalm 81."

When she read it, I, in and out of consciousness, wondered why I was given this Psalm to read. What would this Psalm do for me? Would it take away the pain?

The nurse came by and gave me an oral dosage of the painkiller again. It just wasn't working fast enough. A half an hour had passed since I swallowed the last pills, and I began to doze off again. I could hear June praying, asking God to take the pain and allow me to sleep. I jerked up from the bed, grabbed her by the shirt collar and screamed,

"I can't take this anymore... It hurts! It hurts! It hurts!"

I let go of her shirt, slumped back down into the bed, as if in resignation and began to rock back and forth again. It had only been less than a half hour since the last one. When will this thing end?

Not knowing what to do, June started crying and saying to the Lord,

"Lord, I prayed thirty minutes ago and You haven't answered yet... Please, Lord, take away the pain... Take it away now, please."

I jumped up with such suddenness, that I startled June at first. A pain that was unbearable shot through my body and I screamed. June ran and got the nurse and told him he needed to do something now. He came back with a syringe filled with morphine, I believe, and I was out within seconds to the great la-la-land.

Monday morning came and I woke up to see June cuddled up under a blanket in the lazy-boy chair they had brought in for her. I looked and found that there were a few bruises I had inflicted upon myself when I twisted, turned, and knocked my body against the poles of the bed to ease the pain I was in.

Surgery was pushed back for unknown reasons, and I became scared because my family was not told and were nowhere in sight. I wanted to see them before I went into the operating room, but the doctors couldn't wait until eleven o'clock. Thank God for June who stuck by me the entire time. She was the closest thing to family that I had to reach out to and say a prayer for me.

I woke up from surgery in terrible pain. Things were hanging from all parts of my lower body, and the oxygen tube that was hanging from my nose was burning the mucous membrane I had left in my nostrils. It felt like my nose was on fire.

My doctor appeared at the foot of my bed in the recovery room, squeezed my toes, and said,

"Hewlette, you have your uterus."

I didn't feel any more pain. Not for a hot minute. I was overjoyed. I was in heaven shouting all over God's throne while still under the effects of the anesthesia. If I could at that moment, I would have done some back flips.

"Hallelujah! God did it again!" I was screaming in my mind.

Later that evening, that doctor, who I had not seen in my life before, but who God had pre-ordained to do the surgery, came by to see how I was doing.

"You know what?" he asked. "That tumor was the size of a soccer ball, and weighed close to five pounds."

That's incredible! My brother Aldean, in his own special way said,

"Well Sis, basically, you gave birth today."

As true to life as his statement was, we all just shook our heads in amazement.

"We also found out that if you had not taken the surgery today and had opted to go home, the likelihood of your living today would have been zero," the doctor noted.

My mouth fell ajar as I wondered what took place in the operating room.

"When we went in to remove the tumor, we realized that you had begun to hemorrhage. You would have bled to death if we did not do the surgery today," he said.

Faint? Yes, I nearly did. Can you imagine...holding on to faith, trusting God to move on my behalf, and then later dying from a hemorrhage? What a blow of defeat that would have been. What great questions would have been airlifted to heaven with tears? What sudden impact would my death have on my family, my friends, and the church? What great interruption that would have been in heaven?

Thank God we don't have to answer any of those questions. My family and friends that gathered at my bedside glorified God for His hand in the entire matter. I was delivered with an awesome testimony, but I had questions.

I remember lying in my bed one Saturday morning and having a vivid vision. I had only been home for a about a week and had begun to question God,

"Why did I need to get an operation?"

"Why didn't You just touch my body and heal me?"

You may be thinking who are *you* to ask God such questions. Well, God and I have an ongoing, open relationship that gives me the freedom to approach Him as any daughter would her father.

In the vision, I saw Jesus sitting on the right hand of God. I began to overhear their conversation,

"You know Hewlette expects us to heal her," Jesus said.

"I know, but if I do, the saints will just praise me for a while and then it will all be forgotten," God responded.

As I listened keenly, I saw where God held on to the sides of the throne and began rocking to the left and the right while saying,

"I want to be moved on my throne like this... I want others to be touched to the point of change by her experience."

I laid there with tears flowing down the sides of my face into my ears. Had I truly seen a vision of heaven and overheard God's conversation with His Son? The phone rang and knocked me back to earth's realm.

"Hi Hewlette, can I come by and see you today," a friend asked.

"Sure. That'll be great," I responded.

"Oh by the way, I want you to know that as a result of your faith and ordeal, I decided to recommit my life to the Lord. Me and the kids are going to church tomorrow," she announced.

"Really? That's great," I responded.

"Well, when we left your hospital room, my kids and I began praying for you in the car. And look, God answered our prayers. Your surgery was successful," she added.

The Bible says that all heaven rejoices when a soul gives his or her heart to the Lord. God truly rocked on His throne that day. I believe He rocked, not only that day, but for several weeks before and after the operation. Folks who never prayed before were talking to God on my behalf. The school where I worked was so concerned that the staff made cards and brought gifts. The students even seemed to have held prayer vigils for me. People came together to beg heaven for a miracle.

REFLECTION ON LESSONS LEARNED

←*←*←*←*←*←*←

Nothing in the world could have prepared me for the pain and agony I experienced that cold winter evening. As I look back on it all, I see so many great miracles and carefully orchestrated steps. God had this figured out all along. He wanted to get more than just a "thank you" from this experience. I believe God wanted something that would cause tremors in the camp of the enemy long after the ordeal was over. I believe He was moved for some time.

Not every thing that is painfully wrong is a mistake. What seemed like the worst thing to happen to me became a catalyst in bringing people together. It somewhat reminded me of 9/11. After that incident, no one was afraid of mentioning God or prayer. People looked out for each other.

I learned that when bad things happen, God is still there. My "intimacy scripture" that the Lord gave me several years ago said, *"He shall be call upon me and I will answer him: I will be with him in trouble: I will deliver him, and honour him"* (Psalm 91:15).

He promises never to leave or forsake us. He will never abandon His children as we are His prized possessions. So yes, God is there with us in the midst of our pain, disappointment, and trouble. You name it. He is there. God is there showing that:

- His unfailing love is better than life itself
- He satisfies us with the richest of His provision
- He offers hope through so many difficult situations
- We can sing for joy under His protective wings
- Jesus makes sure we are secure by delivering us with much might

Complete trust is needed to prove the awesome power of God. A blind faith with no ulterior plan will give God no other recourse but to come through for us. Asking with this great faith should bring about a change. I John 5:14-15 says, *"And we are sure of this, that he will listen to us whenever we ask him for anything in line with his will. And if we really know he is listening when we talk to him and make our requests, then we can be sure that he will answer us"* (LB).

How can we say He is great? How do we know that He is mighty? And how can we see Him as a deliverer? It is through our times of test, adversity, conflict, pain, disappoints, and fears. Jesus shows up in a supernatural way and gives us a glimpse of power. Yes, we get to know Him on the road of experience.

Because you and I have been through, we now come out with a testimony. One that is very different from what we started with. God is imparting to us experiential faith! He is setting Himself up to move on His throne, again and again... Just for us.

CHAPTER FIVE

JUST ENOUGH LIGHT FOR THE JOURNEY

"No se puede tapar el sol con un dedo."
Translation: "You can not cover the sun with your thumb."
—Nicaraguan Proverb

The awesome creator of heaven and earth has made this world with such beautiful, unique splendor that everyday we can still marvel at its wonders. Who else could have the imagination to give every snowflake its own individuality? Who has the ability to make the birds fly south for the winter and appear, with singing, at the first flicker and burst of spring?

Who would dare tell the sun to illuminate the earth with just enough heat to bring the warm breeze of summer? And who would dare venture to whisper to the trees so they sway to shed their covering for autumn? Only the omnipotent, omniscient, resplendent, magnanimous Creator and Lover of my soul could do this. What a mighty God!

Like the earth, in our walk with the Lord we often experience seasons. These seasons come to glorify the Most High God and to establish us in a firm footing with Him.

Sometimes seasons bring revelation, quietness, new birth, stability, loss, hope, and joy. But what is most important about seasons is that they come at the time when God wills them to come. Because He is a Father, His care of us is predicated on His love for us. Never will a season last longer than it ought, for He knows what each season will work out, through and in us.

In the times that I have experienced loss, darkness, and pain, God has always sent some level of comfort, some ray of hope, some sudden burst of laughter, and unexpected gifts. Sometimes those gifts were the love and companionship of new friends, a bird stopping at my window to serenade me to a new morning, the hugs I received from children, and a warm comforting smile from a stranger.

Whenever we experience pain, hurt, disappointment, and trouble, we tend to think,

"Why me?

"Why am I going through this again?"

"Is there ever going to be an end?"

Never underestimate the power and presence of God in your life. If we allow Him, He will let you know He is in charge and is working things out in your favor. I have learned that *because* He loves me, I must go through hardship at times. Yet, I know for a fact that it's not to destroy me, but to build the awesome "me" He envisioned from the foundation of the world.

You may be asking, "What is so wonderful about that? How does that fit into "light for the journey?" Well, it may not seem like a joyous thought, but while reflecting, I realized that it was a wonderful light that encouraged me along the way. You are now at a better advantage point than I was. I learned this after going through the storm. You now have it to keep you while you are in or headed into a storm.

Ask yourself this question: How do I become great? Do you have an answer yet? Well, I have one. It's painful! Are you ready for it? Okay. Let's look at Isaiah 48:10: *"Behold, I have refined you, but not as silver; I have tested you in the furnace of affliction"* (NASB). "What? In order for me to be great I have to suffer," you maybe asking yourself silently?

I love this scripture because the Lord gave it to me when I was going through some very rough times in my life. A cursory glance of the verse would lead you to believe that this pathway is constantly poised with suffering. But in looking at it closely, we find that the mere fact that God decides to put us in the furnace of suffering speaks volumes to that fact that He has already willed that we will survive it. Amen!

The refining is not like how silver is broken down in the process and becomes liquefied. No, I am inclined to believe it is more like the process of refining gold—retaining original form, but breaking away needless, heavy unwanted particles.

One cannot see the true worth and value of gold because it comes from the depths and caverns of its hiding place with dross and worthless matter all over it. But as it goes through the refining process, it retains its original form. Everything that is not gold is burned away, thus allowing the true essence of its nature to shine forth.

When we are placed in "our" furnace of suffering, there are things, circumstances, situations, and people God is trying to eradicate from our lives. He wants our true purity and fullness to shine forth. He does not get joy from a speck of light when the potential is there for a ray to come bursting through the darkness. No, He wants His fullness to shine forth so that the beauty that has always been a part of you can break forth and others can benefit from "your" light and His glory.

In my life, the refining brought about a great promotion. Never in the existence of my church had a female been ordained as a minister. Well, my church broke away from tradition and ventured into the realm of spiritual maturity. My time in the furnace proved to be rewarding in many ways.

Not only did I gain more than what I lost in the "process," but also received a double portion of His anointing to do His will and perform the tasks He assigns me. I gained great favor in the eyes of my Pastor and other leaders and was promoted to positions of honor.

I truly have been showered by God's favor. Having never paid attention to it until I was faced with difficulties, I witnessed the unconditional love of God move in my life. He stretched his hand forth and moved beyond the bars of my despair and touched the hearts of people far and near to bless me in ways that blew the logic of it right out of my head.

Sometimes when good things happen to us, we begin to assess just how we came by that great thing. We may think,

"Oh yeah, I remember when I helped out so and so."

Or we may say,

"This happened because I prayed for this or that."

Well, sorry to burst both your bubble and mine. Those wonderful great, small, and in-between things we received of the Lord were as a result of His great <u>FAVOR</u>. It was given without any deed on our part. It was poured out without us impressing Him to do so. Favor was given without regard for race, color or creed, and accepted without knowledge of its coming. Yes, God's favor is great towards us.

I remember going to church one Saturday. I entered my car and realized that my gas tank gauge read "empty." I only live five miles away from church, but I was afraid to drive my car because I forgot how long I had been riding around with it on empty. I "looked to the hills from whence cometh my help" and said, "God, please get me to church." Oh and by the way, did I tell you I only had two dollars in my pocketbook and that was earmarked for offering? Well, that's all I had, not a penny more.

The church service was wonderful that day, the Lord moved mightily among us, and His presence could be felt. As we approached the time of sharing, I could feel a whimpering spirit come over me. It was as if it came out of nowhere and found a place to rest—right on my heart.

"It's offering time," the moderator announced.

Everyone began to cheer and clap with excitement. I sat still with my head down. Why? Well had I begun to think,

"If I give my last two dollars, my car is going to shut off on me... I need this for gas... God understands... He knows my situation..."

I knew that praise wasn't about to fill up the tank, so if this money was coming out of my pocketbook, it was walking out of there to the gas tank. I had to use my God-given common sense. Or so I thought.

The offering plate moved its way toward me. I felt I had to at least look like I had offering. You know how we do it in church—hold our hand like there is something in the middle of it, sit a little bit toward the edge of the bench like we're eagerly awaiting the plate, and smile like God was coming to get that offering from you in person.

Well, I put my hand in that plate like I was dropping a million dollars in it. It was only two dollars. Yes! Yes! Yes! I wrestled the money from its resting place and gave it. I thought nothing more of what I had just done.

After spending some time with the saints—eating, laughing, and sharing—I decided to leave for the evening. As I made my way to the "empty gas tanked" car, a friend said,

"Hewlett, do you have gas money?" It kind of caught me off guard so I quickly responded,

"Yeah, I'm okay."

"I didn't ask you if you were okay. I asked if you have gas money?" she scolded.

"Mmmmm, no I don't," I responded with fear and hesitation. She looked at her husband and said,

"Give Hewlette $20 dollars!"

He turned and looked at her with surprise and said,

"She said she's okay!"

The power of a woman, especially a wife, is strong. A look was all he needed. Within seconds, her husband walked over to me and gave me the money from his wallet. Praise God for the Abigails in the church!

There I stood in amazement. I didn't think of the last two dollars I gave for offering as I did not give it cheerfully. My initial response was, "Wow!" God gave me enough money to fill the tank and treat myself to dinner (McDonald's) that night.

Did I do anything to have been blessed that evening? No, I didn't. As a matter of fact, I wrestled with the money in my pocketbook—putting my hands on it, taking my hands off—and wanted it, this inanimate object, to hide away from the reach of my fingers. I knew to give the money was the right thing to do, but I was surely hoping it would just do me a favor and hide.

I realized that God had ordained something greater to happen that day: I would get the opportunity to know Him as my Jehovah Jireh—the God that provides. Could I see it at first? No, because my eyes were only focused on the "now" of my situation. I was preoccupied with the <u>emptiness</u> of my gas tank and not on the <u>fullness</u> of God's love and provision. Looking back, I see that although I gave, it was done begrudgingly and not in a cheerful manner. Thank the Lord for His forgiveness. He truly looked beyond my fault that afternoon and met my need.

No one can ever make me doubt God's ability to do the impossible. I truly mean that! I've had things happen to me that seem to have come right out of left field.

"Money rules the world," I've been told, and I know that a large part of that is true. You cannot go to a clothing store without money. You cannot buy food without money. You cannot buy fine jewelry without money. You cannot pay bills without money. And you definitely cannot go on vacation to top resort areas without money. Well, guess what? I did!

God has blessed me with wonderful friends who have taken me shopping to buy any amount of clothing and shoes I've desired (of course I used wisdom). And there were times that they purchased the clothes, gift wrapped them, and sent them to me. Did I have money? No! Did I look destitute, busted up, and homeless? No! But God sent enough light to cheer me on my journey. I honor and bless Him right now for all He's done and is doing. Hallelujah!

God blessed me with two dear couples that have sowed bountifully into my life. He used them to allow me the opportunity to experience the finer things in life. I have been on vacation to resorts where people were rolling in the dough. And I've received gifts that would probably put some of us in debt. I mean I have cruised with the best of the best, ate with the fattest of the fattest, and had spending money left over (that was given to me, of course).

What was God showing me here? Many of the things I worked to achieve and acquire were not granted to me while I was making over $30,000 dollars a year. No. He brought them to me when I was struggling, living from my little paycheck to paycheck, and trying to pay off school and car loans. God was showing me that He is able to meet all my needs and desires.

There have been many times, I'm sure, where God has laughed at me. I believe some of those times to be when I was a busy making plans for myself.

"Okay, when I'm this age I'll travel here… When I get this amount of money I'll buy that or do this…" I thought to myself.

But God was patiently using His little eraser, wiping them out one by one, and writing His own will for my life. I imagine Him writing,

"No, not yet... When you don't have a job I'll give you this... When you're low on funds I'll furnish this for you... When you are alone I'll comfort you this way... What you are looking for is right here... If you trust Me I'll take care of this for you..."

Don't you just love when He takes over and does the thing Himself? Okay, I'll admit, it doesn't feel good at first because my timetable seems to work just fine, at least from where I sit. But later on I find out that His way is always best. Our hindsight ability is very clear and we see that His plans were perfect.

Speaking of God laughing, I've had my own times of laughter. Some things that happened to me along the way up the mountain were side-splittingly funny. Others just warranted a good laugh. Like the time I went to Brooklyn, New York to preach.

I had prepared what I thought to be a powerful sermon to encourage and excite the people. I was dressed like the typical Pentecostal female preacher—long-sleeved hip-length Evan Picone jacket, ankle-length designer skirt, my mother's broad felt hat, and a handkerchief to flash out at the appropriate time.

The atmosphere was set and I had a very captivated audience. I began to preach about Jeremiah's trip to the potter's house. The "Amen's!" and "Praise the Lord's!" were coming from the people. Some stood up occasionally and waved their hands. Others sat, listening and watching intently.

As I moved about the platform, with microphone in my right hand, I was nearing the middle of my sermon when I felt something shift. I kept speaking, but my mind wondered in a flash, "What was that?"

The attention of the audience seemed to be glued to my every word. I continued to walk about the platform while flailing my left hand. Then suddenly, I felt a pulling, a moving... Something was falling from beneath my skirt.

Fear gripped me like the grasp of a hungry bear, and I slapped the lower left part of my hip. This seemed as no big deal to the audience as they are accustomed to various gyrations by preachers. As I slapped my hip I felt the waist of what I thought was my pantyhose.

"Dear God, don't tell me this is happening? I thought to myself.

"No way! Not here! Not in front of all these people!"

Incredibly enough, I continued to preach. No one knew what was happening. The "Amen's!" and "Hallelujahs!" kept coming, and members of the audience began to express joy and excitement as I explained the scripture. I decided not to move around as much for fear of it just falling. I grabbed the side of my skirt and began holding what I thought to be the waist of my pantyhose.

Now I knew I had attired myself properly—making sure everything was in place and meeting the standards of the pastor who invited me to speak—but something most troubling, most provocative, and most embarrassing was taking place. I continued preaching and still no one suspected anything.

I decided to station my self in one spot—right behind the podium—just in case something tragic would happen, but it began to move again. I held on to it for dear life, but it seemed this thing had a mind of its own. It partially stayed in place where I held it, but it began to slip down on my right hip. I continued preaching and still no one suspected anything.

As I ventured to the climax of my message, the people were all in tune with their eyes fastened intently on me. The organist was poised at the threshold of doing the right moves on the keys. I knew I was about to get a loud amen—I felt it.

This "thing" made its way down pass my right hip to the middle of my thigh. "Is it really my pantyhose? Did my camisole pop?" I asked myself while preaching. I held onto the thing for dear life at the middle side of my left thigh. I kept preaching, reaching the people, and hanging onto their "Amen's!" and "Hallelujahs!" But still, no one suspected anything.

I looked to my left from the pulpit and the musicians (all males) were listening and watching me intently. I looked to my right and the Pastor and other Elders were fixed on me and the message. I looked in front of me and without appropriate segue said,

"Church, Oh Church!"

"Yes!" They responded with exuberance.

"I tell you, I feel like David… I feel just like when David rejoiced at the return of the Ark of God, and I, too, rejoice!" I exclaimed.

"Yes!" "Thank you, Jesus!" "Amen!" "Hallelujah!" reverberated from the audience.

The room seemed to be charged with electricity as folks popped up and down as if their names were being called for a prize. What took place next was simply unbelievable, yet gracious. With a charge of energy and without knowing the outcome, I shouted,

"I rejoice like David. He rejoiced until he danced out of his clothes. I rejoice 'cause I'm coming out of my slip!"

I stepped to my right, let go of this thing I held onto under my skirt, and "Whooosh!" it fell. Donna, a good friend of mine, ran up to the pulpit at breakneck speed, grabbed the embarrassing garb, placed it under her arm, ran back to her seat, plopped it into her purse, and resumed listening as if no embarrassing act just took place.

The roar that came from the audience was truly mixed. Some stood up and cheered, others laughed and began praising the Lord; the rest were overcome by shock.

Well, needless to say, I continued preaching like nothing out of the ordinary happened. The church truly came alive. It seemed the whole place lit up more from that incident than from my preaching.

Word traveled like a wild conflagration (fire). By the time I made it back home and attended my church on the weekend, my Pastor greeted me with, "Well, say there, Sister Hewlette, I heard you preached right out of your clothes in New York."

Laughter is great. I think it is one of the best gifts God has given us. Proverbs 17:22 says, *"A merry heart doeth good like medicine: but a broken spirit drieth the bones."* Laughter brings life to your body and excites those areas that need a jumpstart. A sad and broken spirit will sap what little strength you have left. Laughter also helps to give us a healthier perspective on things. Maybe if we laughed more, the problems we face wouldn't seem as difficult to endure. Try laughing. It does work. It's also a ray of light and hope that God shines on your journey.

How about laughing at this one...?

I complain often to my friends and family about guys in cars who have nothing else to do with their horns but to blow them at me. I mean come on? I know I'm a good looking, highly favored, blessed sister in the Lord. But, a sister has better things to do with her time that to turn around, find out which car, and what guy wants to interrupt her intimate time with the Lord, her time to make her mental list of things to do, or her time to put ideas together for her next book. Come on now!

Look, I used to respond to those annoying car horns 'cause I thought it was someone I knew. Well, I don't any more. No Sir! I refuse to be taken in. I will not continue to be interrupted, humiliated, and disgusted by old men with little or no teeth!

Now see there... Go ahead and laugh!!!

CHAPTER SIX

I'M UP TO HERE WITH PROBLEMS!

*"No man can ever impress another man and lead him
out of the depths unless he himself has met God in a dark
cloud. It is not enough that one should merely speak
to God; he must see Him in a storm."*
—Bishop Fulton J. Sheen

Why don't things work out the way I expect them?
I'm living a righteous life. What's going on? Why
is it when I make a step forward something happens, I find
myself being catapulted three steps backward? Why can't I
see a little ways up in the future so I can make the adjust-
ments or brace myself for what's coming?

I wish I could answer these questions as poignantly as
I ask them, but my experiences have taught me that every
situation demands of me something unique, something that
I had not realized existed in or outside of me. Every situation speaks loudly of a different outcome for the betterment
of me.

I had just driven up to my front gate when the drizzle that
had followed me home that night was now becoming full-

blown raindrops. As I ventured to turn off my headlights, I realized that my usual greeter had not jumped the fence to welcome me. A few feet in front of my car sat Raspus, our family cat, with tail hidden. Intrigued by the fact that he sat under a car motionless and refused to do his usual thing — walk with me up the steps and wait patiently as I rustle through my pocketbook to find the house keys — caused me to sit there for a while, just starring.

I turned on the high beam a few times to get a response, but he didn't even turn his head to look in my direction, not even a flicker of a tail or a twitch of the ear. What on earth had this cat's attention? What was so important that he could not fulfill his furry duties?

A few more flicker of my high beams revealed a powerful reflection. I sat in amazement at the sight of two glassy green, dark brown eyes peering just a little outside the silhouette of Raspus' figure. Yes, it was a female cat! Her grace and "purrability" captured his attention, so much so that greeting me did not matter anymore.

Unlike my cat, Raspus, who sat focused and poised for something wonderful, I could not handle the silence. Being still, along with the alone time — no one and no thing around to amuse me — was pretty difficult to bear. I wanted to hear God's voice, I wanted to feel His touch, and I needed to know He was there. Like a manipulative child, I pouted and squirmed for His attention. I had forgotten His words to me, "When you can't feel me, know that I am there."

Did that matter? No. I needed to know, without a shadow of a doubt, that God was standing there beside me. God is truly amazing! I demanded His attention and I needed it now. I did not know that near tragedies would let me see that He was truly there. I didn't know that always zeroing in on "my" world would let me miss the opportunity to reach out to a friend.

It was a wonderful summer day and I had made all the preparations for the trip to Virginia Beach. I traveled with a friend and the youth group from her church. We sang songs, played games, and chat all the way down Interstate I-95.

We found a wonderful spot on the beach, just a few feet from the ripples of the waves, and set up our temporary vacation spot. As far as the eyes could see, beach umbrellas of every color and size decorated the white and gray-sanded beach. The sounds of the waves crashing against the shore, along with seagulls and the melodious sound of little children screaming, playing, and chasing each other helped to set the tone for a picturesque day.

We had been in the water for a few hours and without an announcement, we all ran from the water and converged on the beach for lunch. That act alone seemed to have been orchestrated by the spirit of hunger...true hunger. We ate and some of us took a quick afternoon nap.

"Hey guys, let's go ride the waves," someone exclaimed.

The announcement seemed to burst the solitude I had crawled into for a few minutes. I found myself shielding my eyes from the strong rays of the sun while picking the grains of sand from my upper arms left there by scattering feet racing to the water.

"Come on, Hewie, let's go," someone hollered.

I carefully rose to the call. I checked out my swim attire to make sure I was fully clad with my "Joseph coat of many colors" looking swimsuit. I quickly brushed the rest of the sand off my body and gingerly walked on my tippy toes to the water while avoiding the shells, bottle caps, twigs, blankets, bags, chairs, heads, hands, feet, and other plain old beach stuff.

Now mind you, I don't know how to swim, but I had learned how to ride the waves the year before on vacation in Myrtle Beach. When I entered the water, it chilled my body. Yes it did! I hesitated and wondered if I should turn back, but, seeing all the fun my friends were having up ahead of me, I braved the cold chilly water of Virginia.

The initial steps I took brought the water to my waist. I had gone for some time with it at that level, but as I ventured closer to where my friends were I realized that the water was moving, moving in the wrong direction—up my body. It was now at my shoulders and so I froze. Yes, I froze out of fear. Fear I felt way deep down in my bones. I believe my bones started trembling out of fear for itself. I could hear a voice in my head saying,

"No, don't do it. Don't go any further."

"Come on, Hew, just a few more steps and the water will go back down. Come on, you can do it! Don't be scared," came from the crowd.

Their words drowned out the soft prompting I heard in my head, so I ventured on. The water did get lower as I continued walking and wading towards my group of friends. It was now at my torso, so all the fear I was experiencing begun to fade away.

We played all sorts of made-up water games—underwater Olympic dancing, dodge ball, etc. Big ships and jet skiers went by in the distance. This caused waves in the area where we played, so we would ride out the wave for the distance. This went on for about two hours then some of us began to get weary.

"Let's go back to shore," someone said.

However, the majority was not in favor so we continued playing. A few minutes went by and then someone hollered,

"Let's ride this wave back to shore!"

I turned and saw this gigantic wave that seemed to be the size of Mount St. Helen with its ruffles of foam churning and stirring as if it needed to bellow out its content on land. I had no fear 'cause I had experience riding waves. We positioned ourselves as if in a race waiting for the signal of the gun.

Whoosh! Splash! The wave came in with such force that it knocked us against each other; we lost all sense of balance. I began reaching, grabbing for something to hold onto. Kicking, kicking, kicking for dear life, I tried to touch the bottom of the water with my feet, but nothing was there.

Peering through the murky waters, I saw some of my friends fighting to get to shore, but they soon realized that I was far from them. Whoosh! Another large wave came and dragged me further out to sea. I kicked, I slapped, I gulped, I kicked, I slapped, and I gulped. I began to lose control of my arms now; my body began to tire.

As I began to sink I cried aloud in my head,

"God, you didn't say I was gonna die this way, You didn't!"

Whoosh! Splash! Another wave came and slapped the back of my body lunging me forward beneath its grasp. I kicked, I kicked, and I kicked! I threw my hands in the air to holler for help, but it was silenced by a large gulp of sandy salt water.

Another wave came by and lifted my body upward. I angled my head where my face and the sky kissed each other. I took in as much air to go down for the last time, then, I went under.

My kick slowed down now and I began to wrestle in my spirit. Wrestling with thoughts of life and death, my body became limp and I began to sink, sink, sink... I could see each grain of sand in front of me, now, and each seaweed and rubble. It was as if time was going by quickly, but in slow motion. As I held my breath for the last time my body began to descend, down, down, down...

"I haven't done all you want me to do," I said with a voice of resignation in my head.

"You didn't tell me I was gonna go this way, God," I cried.

I could feel the tears in my eyes distinctly from the water that was now becoming my grave. My heart pained as I tried to maneuver the air between my chest and my throat.

That's it! I'm dying. I let out my last bit of air and my body went on automatic pilot. I began to ingest water as my body began to fight. Fight... Fight... Fight...

The next thing I remember seeing were all these eyes. Eyes that seemed to be bulging from faces around me, staring and asking, "Are you okay? Hewlette, can you understand what we're saying?"

I heard them, but I could not respond. It was the faces of those who rescued me from the watery grave: Augustus Reece, Rohan May, and Howard Reece. I tried, really tried to talk, but I couldn't give a coherent response to their questions, nor thank them then. I was still in shock, and my body was still not yet mine. My hands and legs were limp; mucous ran from my eyes, nose, and mouth.

The doctor came by to check my vital signs. He insisted on pumping my stomach, but I wouldn't allow it. When I came to full consciousness, I cried like a baby right there on that beach in the spot where they put me to sit up. I sat there as if I was the only one on the beach with no one else left in the world.

Nightmares plagued me for several days after that. I remember driving home alone the next day from Baltimore. I was in the left lane musing on the events of the weekend when I looked up in my rear-view mirror and saw a hearse traveling behind me on the right. As it drove alongside me, with a red oak casket draped in baby's breath and yellow roses, I began crying.

I could barely see to get home after that. I cried, I cried, I cried. I imagined my body being escorted back to Washington, D.C. from Baltimore, Maryland. I imagined the pain and agony my family and friends would go through.

I won't tell you what happened when I told my mother. I'll leave that to your imagination. I will tell you, though, that when I went to Tuesday night prayer meeting and told my Pastor the story, he cried and magnified God.

That next weekend in church, my Pastor prior to delivering his sermon, stood up before the congregation and said, "Saints, we have someone in our midst today who God brought back from the dead..."

He looked at me and beckoned for me to come to the front of the church. He handed me the microphone, and I told the church my story. Some listened with amazement, some cried, and others praised and worshipped the Lord.

My Pastor hit the nail right on the head! I am someone that God has brought back from the dead. I didn't die (all the way), but He brought me back from natural and spiritual death and gave me a new perspective on life.

You see, before that experience, I was only concerned about my situation and me. I had begun to complain about not having money to buy exactly what I wanted. I had begun to look at all that my friends and former colleagues had going for them. I started measuring my past against my present condition and loathed the fact that I was not able to do the stuff I was used to doing.

I forgot. I forgot. I forgot. I truly forgot the pledge I had made to Him one Sunday night at a worship service about six months prior. He had whispered in my ear that night,

"Read Psalm 78..."

I did it right then and there and an assurance came rushing into my heart.

"Promise me you will not think that I have forgotten you, or are far from you. Promise me you'll remember that I'll always provide for you even when you can't see or feel me."

"Yes Lord, I will. Help me to do it, Lord," I said.

"satan is going to try and let you think otherwise, but know I am with you," the voice of the Lord said to me.

Oh, when I got home, I read the story again and told Him that I would not be like the Children of Israel who saw His mighty hand in Egypt, walked on dry ground in the middle of the Red Sea, had 24 hour 7 days a week protection from their enemies, dined on angel food with quail every day, drank sweet water in the middle of a desert, and never had to purchase another change of clothing or shoes for the entire forty years they lived in the wilderness, *but* still complained about how God didn't care about them.

I forgot. So God, in His infinite mercy, gave me another chance to remember. And remember I did...

REFLECTION ON LESSONS LEARNED

←*←*←*←*←*←*←

There are many lessons I learned from this entire ordeal. I found out things about "Hewlette and friendships" that pushed me to make necessary steps in the right direction. I share some of them with you here.

My cat, Raspus, taught me a wonderful lesson: *"Be still and know that I am God..."* (Psalm 46:10). In life's struggles, we find that sometimes God calms the storm and other times He calms His child. My cat was focused on what was in front of him and was not distracted or moved by the intermittent flashing of my high beams, nor by the fact that it had begun to rain harder.

He was calm, cool, and collected without a worry or care. He knew that he had a warm home to run to when he was ready to come in. Yes, I was someone familiar, but my association with him did not matter at that time. There was something more important that warranted his attention.

As I was writing the story of my near drowning experience, I stopped in the middle of the sentence, "God, you didn't say I was gonna die this way, You didn't!" and cried like a baby. I was reliving it all over again; it brought back so much physical and emotional pain.

For several months it bothered me that the incident occurred and there were no warnings prior to my getting to the beach. But then out of the blue, I remembered there was a word, a warning I received, but I did not apply it to that trip.

I remembered arguing with God about it. Yes, you heard me correctly, I argued with God about it. See, a friend of mine had invited me and I did not want to disappoint her as she had said that I had not supported her and the youth department in a good while. I had been invited on other trips prior to that one and had turned each of them down.

It had been sometime now and I thought the "grace period" was up. You see, the Lord had me in a season of stillness. I was encouraged months earlier by the Lord not to go anywhere. But I went because it was someone I was close to and it was a church outing. Needless to say, I cried out to the Lord and asked Him to forgive me when I realized that my disobedience nearly cost me my life.

Well, like I said before, my cat taught me a great lesson:

- Remain focused on those things that matter. Interruptions, distractions, chaos, and fright may come, but fix your eyes on the prize.
- Do not to put the voice of a friend, co-worker, lover, etc. over the voice of God. Let the voice of God be louder and more pronounced than that of another. I wanted to please a friend rather than walk in obedience to the Lover and Keeper of my soul.

Other lessons I learned are:

- Even when we mess up, Jesus is still there interceding on our behalf. Hebrews 7:25 says, *"Wherefore He is able to save them to the uttermost that come unto God by Him, seeing He ever liveth to make intercession for them."*
- When I was not faithful in keeping with my end of the promise, He remained faithful. Jeremiah writes in Lamentation 3:22-23, *"It is of the Lord's mercies*

*that we are not consumed, because His compassions
fail not. They are new every morning: great is Thy
faithfulness."*

- I realized that I had a purpose on this earth and God
  was not about to let the devil have his way. I was
  created to do great things in the kingdom of God, and
  I was just on the threshold of realizing my potential.
- Your testimony becomes a story of praise that helps
  to lift others out of the depths of despair. See God
  using your situation to bless you and others. Don't
  be silent about it; tell about the goodness of God.
  *"Let the redeemed of the Lord say so, whom He
  hath redeemed from the hand of the enemy"* (Psalm
  107:2).

I don't know what areas of your life may be causing you
pain or disappointment, but do this for me—don't give up on
God for He loves you. Be tenacious in your pursuit of Him.
Hold on for dear life.

Can I take a moment to relate a short story to you? Okay,
thanks.

It was a cool and bleak November afternoon. I had
stopped by a friend's house to drop off some soup my Mom
had made. I was only there for about fifteen minutes. As I
made my way back home down Route 50 to Interstate 95, I
checked my left side mirror for clearance to change lanes.

It was then that I realized that I had an unwanted
passenger. There was a black spider, about three-fourths the
size of a dime, holding on to the mirror as I drove sixty-five
miles per hour. I thought to open my window and pluck him
off, but decided to turn on my windshield washer fluid and
spray him off the side of the glass instead. Needless to say
that did not work.

Plan two was initiated—increase my speed down Route
50. Seventy, seventy-five, eighty, ninety-five... Yes, I broke
the speed limit to rid my car of this annoying creature. I

feared it would eventually get between the panels of my door and come inside the car. But to my dismay, it held on. It did not move, flinch a muscle, or bat an eye. It held on, held on to its original position as if it had been glued on as an ornament.

When I reached my destination, it took off and ran between the door panels as I had expected. I quickly opened the door, jumped from the car, and watched it crawl right into the lower panel near my parking brake. I mustered up enough courage to locate this creepy, crawly creature and put it to rest.

Okay, why the story? Well, I believe it conveys just how important it is to hold on. No matter what happens around you or to you. Yes, we make mistakes. We even turn our backs on Him at times. But a promise is a promise. Keep your end of it because He's sure to keep His end of the promise.

You want to bet? Hope you have lots of money because you are guaranteed to lose if you don't listen. Okay, good! That's right. Go ahead, listen to God and trust Him with all your heart. He is the faithful God.

CHAPTER SEVEN

STRETCHED TO THE POINT OF FORGIVENESS

*"He who cannot forgive others destroys the bridge
over which he himself must pass."*
—George Herbert

Whoa! Screech! Stop! That's what the wheels of our mind do when we are confronted with forgiveness. It appears that indelible skid marks are imposed upon our thoughts when we are confronted with having to forgive someone.

"What! I have to do what?" you say to yourself when someone comes to you and say, "You hurt me and it's time you own up to what you've done. Forgiveness is in order… I'm waiting…" But as your mind wrestles with this confrontation, you say to yourself, "Hmmmm, the last time I checked, the hurt was inflicted on me."

I have been there and have done that! Maybe for you it did not happen that way, but some part of it may very well mirror your situation. Reading it may have even sent a ripple shock throughout your body that still seems to resonate at the least mention of forgiveness.

Now, it seems I have an overwhelming vote on this chapter, especially for those of us who go through storms. This book would not be complete without addressing that one thing that can be a nemesis for some of us at times. How we react within the realm of forgiveness during the storm sets the course for the next step we will take.

When you are confronted with situations that you know without a shadow of a doubt you did not do, but you are being accused of doing, how do you react? Don't answer yet; let's talk a little.

As you already know, I grew up in a God-fearing home with parents who set concrete examples for us to follow. Now mind you my brothers and I never claimed to be saints as kids, but we tried to imitate what we saw our parents do. Yes, we got into quarrels and some physical fights, but it seemed we always ended up making peace at the end of the day or a day or two after. I think it's because our parents' hands of justice reached beyond the line of demarcation we had erected between our friendship and family-hood, yanked us back into the reality of family, and knocked some God-fearing sense back into us.

I know for me it always seemed they knew when we were not talking to each other. Questions were answered abruptly, no looking out for each other with chores, and there were no giggles or lively talks in the bedrooms as they are accustomed to hearing. Basically, when we were not speaking to each other, the house told on us. It bellowed a quietness that alarmed the matriarch of the family—Mother.

In order to avoid questions, we forgave each other because we had to. We had no choice in the matter. If we did not, we would definitely feel the consequences—everyone would. Anyway, as kids, we loved doing things together so making up was easier than it is now. As we got older, it became a bit harder, but we still had the "Matriarch" to deal with, so forgiveness was done quite quickly.

Just telling you about my childhood reminds me of one such incident. I do not remember all the specifics that lead up to my fight with my eldest brother, Glen, but I remember him pushing me and walking away. I, being the shortest in stature, reacted with the force of an Olympian throwing a discus. I picked up a carton of milk from the kitchen table, walked through the accordion pleated kitchen door, positioned myself for the optimal result, threw back my right arm, and released the object with acute precision.

Needless to say my brother, the big target, anticipated my retaliation and ducked. Down the eggshell white painted wall of our foyer bled white vitamin D milk and at the base of the wall sat an exploded carton box. Glen stood there with a grin that infuriated me further.

How did it end? I don't remember, but I do remember begging him not to tell Mommy. I even remember asking him for some money a couple days later, so we must have had some type of discourse to get me to the point of begging for funds. I am inclined to believe that I ended up saying, "Glen, sorry for throwing the milk at you."

I shared that story with you to show just how quick we were to forgive when we were children. There were no rehashing of the story, no drawing a great big picture to show how much hurt was inflicted, and no long tape recording to rehearse the sword-riddled words. We knew we had to get over this because there would be greater consequences if our parents found out. But more importantly for us, we needed closure for the happiness we always shared and gave to each other.

We needed each other for many things: bargaining for chore duty; helping with homework; getting together on Friday nights and playing gospel records and tapes while banging on trashcan bottoms, pillows, and strumming on an old guitar my Dad gave to Glen; keeping our stories—I mean lies—straight whenever we had to face Mother; and laughing into the wee hours of the night on the weekends.

Quarrels and fights got in the way of all of that. And it was not a good feeling being alone in your room listening to music. Our house was always alive with sounds of laughter and music. The only thing that changed that atmosphere was when one of us was angry with the other. Looking back at it all, I truly see how much forgiveness played a major role in the joys we experienced as kids.

Now I know that my childhood spats and quarrels cannot be compared to the hurt that you have experienced. But I share it with you to amplify the importance of forgiveness in our every-day lives. Our success depends on it! Our happiness is predicated on it! Our relationship with God and each other is built on it! And the door to our Father's presence is opened by it!

I could share countless stories with you about the pain and the sorrow I experienced at the hands of those who I cherished as dear friends, colleagues, and church brethren. But in my experience, I found that not one person was to be blamed for my hurt. My hurt, pain, sorrow, tears, anguish, and disappointment were the result of two persons—the individual I considered the aggressor and myself.

I found out later in life that "hurting people hurt other people." It was not the first time I was hurt; it would not be the last time. I hurt people at times and you hurt people at times. Sometimes it is not intentional, but because of where we are in our private pain: a wrong word is said, a strange look is given, a bad deed is done, and the correct emotion is not expressed.

In general, especially in the body of Christ, we hurt each other unintentionally. Our response to the injury compounds the matter so much so that by the time the dust settles, the pinhole injury we've received is now a gaping machete wound. Granted, some times you have individuals who are revengeful to the point that they strategize how and when they will inflict the next wound. But forgiveness still has to be extended to those persons.

I do not want you to think that I do not understand the pain and how hard it is sometimes to forgive. Believe me, I do understand. But it is satan's desire that we hold on to our pain and nurse it. Why? Well, that way he can keep you and me from entering a place of power. I am encouraged to share with you the awesome power that God has given each of us to release each other from a debt of wrongs.

Let's look at this three-syllable word for a moment. For-give-ness. The Oxford Reference Dictionary defines forgive: "to cease to feel angry or resentful towards (a person) or about (an offense), to pardon, to remit (a debt)." [The Oxford Reference Dictionary, (New York, 1986), "forgive."] The "ness" portion of the word simply means the act or the state of being forgiven.

There is a great release of freedom that is activated in forgiveness. But, we place ourselves in bondage and become a prisoner in the diabolical scheme of satan when we do not forgive. The harboring of un-forgiveness brings us to a state of anger, resentment, hate, and bitterness. They begin to eat at the very core of who we are. We become dry and brittle inside, to where the least unkind word spoken to us breaks us into pieces of deeper hurt and anger.

Un-forgiveness eventually leads us to isolation. We no longer feel comfortable being around people as we think no one understands or can empathize with our condition. So we create our own little world and talk only to those who have been hurt like us and are stuck in their pain and resentment.

Living in the "city of un-forgiveness" leaves us existing on meager nourishment. As a result, we become emaciated, weak, and open to the snares and darts of satan. Whenever he feels like it, he yanks that chain of resentment, anger, and pain to the point where we begin to relive the hurtful moments over and over again. The tapes in our head just won't stop playing those hurtful words, those wickedly devised schemes, and the sharp cuts to our emotions.

And so we view the landscape of our condition while sitting on the porch of resentment. We sit there, rocking in the chair of revenge, fanning the flames of anger, drinking from the cup of bitterness, and watching our life ebb away in the city of un-forgiveness.

There is no true life in this city — No laughter, no sounds of children playing in the streets, no birds singing a beautiful morning tune, no relatives stopping by for social gatherings, and no invitations to birthday parties, weddings, baby showers, etc. The only action in town is the movie, "I Remember What You Did to Me." Occasionally, old slewfoot (satan) breaks up the monotony of that flick with "I'm Gonna Get You Back If It's the Last Thing I Do." There is no life at all in this God-forsaken city.

Realizing the devastating effects of un-forgiveness, why do we find ourselves living there sometimes? Is it worth our happiness? Is it more important than the love and fellowship we shared with the person? Are we allowing it to replace the warmth of our hearts? Is it more important than our relationship with Jesus Christ? Is it greater than the awesome destiny God has ordained for our lives?

Oh to laugh and sing again! Oh to appreciate the sheer glow and feel of the warmth of the sun against my face! Imagine the sound of the caroling birds afoot my window! What joy to hear the waves dash against the rocks while squeezing the water-soaked sand between my toes! What formidable sensation to feel the gentle touch of a baby's little hand on the zenith of my cheek! And what awesome refreshing feeling to experience the hug of a friend's warm embrace!

Yes, this and more is what we miss out on when we decided to harbor negative feelings towards another person and exhibit un-forgiveness. That person we cared about,

laughed with, ate with, talked with, and worshipped with
needs us. He or she may not realize it, but we know that
somewhere deep inside of us there is a need to be one again.
For only by us can the person experience the release necessary to walk in victory.

You and I are not the only ones that go through storms of
emotional pain and anguish. From the time Adam and Eve
sinned in the Garden of Eden, humankind has been experiencing injury and pain. If King David were here today,
he would gladly sit us down and tell us his story. In Psalm
55:12-14; 20-21 he says,

> *"It was not an enemy that taunted me—then I could
> have borne it; I could have hidden and escaped. But
> it was you, a man like myself, my companion and
> my friend. What fellowship we had, what wonderful
> discussions as we walked together to the Temple of
> the Lord on holy days. This friend of mine betrayed
> me—I who was at peace with him. He broke his prom-
> ises. His words were oily smooth, but in his heart
> was war. His words were sweet, but underneath were
> dagger"* (LB).

David understood what it meant to be hurt by someone
he cared about and with whom he had sweet fellowship. But
more importantly, David recognized that the hurt he was
experiencing could be lifted, lifted by God alone. In verse
23 he said, *"Give your burden to the Lord, He will carry
them."* In essence, David is saying to us, "Give your pain,
your hurt, your tears, and your disappointment to the Lord.
He will take care of you."

So, instead of us carrying our brother, sister, friend, wife,
husband, father, mother, boss, co-worker, etc. in our hearts,
let the Lord do the carrying instead. He is much stronger than

you or me. He came to set us free from every burden—even the ones we lift up and put on our own shoulders.

Yes, David was truly hurt by someone he cared about, but he also inflicted pain and injury on someone else. In the 11th chapter of 2 Samuel, we find that David awoke from an afternoon nap, went walking on the roof of the palace, saw a beautiful woman taking a bath, and lusted after her. He made inquiries to find out who she was. He found that she was married to Uriah, a Hittite, a faithful soldier in Israel's army and one of David's famous "Thirty" mighty men (see 2 Samuel 23:29 and I Chronicles 11:41).

Although David knew she was the wife of a trusted and faithful soldier, he gave in to his lustful desires and sent messengers to bring her to him. When she arrived at the palace, he brought her into his chamber and had sexual intercourse with her. She later sent word to David to let him know that she was pregnant.

In order to cover up his adulterous act, David sent word to Joab, his captain on the battlefield, and requested the presence of Uriah at the palace. David tried to let it appear that he only wanted to know how the army was getting along and how the war was progressing. After getting this information from Uriah, he encouraged him to go home and relax and sleep with his wife. David even sent a gift to Uriah after he left the palace.

But to the amazement of David, Uriah had not done as he was told. As a matter of fact, he did not even leave the palace. Uriah slept at the palace entrance with some of King David's servants.

"Why didn't you go home, Uriah. You've been away for some time now. Surely you must miss your wife, the softness of her touch, the smell of your soft perfumed bed," David probably said to him? But Uriah, according to the scripture, thought it unfair to enjoy the luxuries of home while his comrades are living in tents and sleeping in the open fields.

After such a profound and admirable response from Uriah, one would think that David would immediately order that the palace be cleared of all his subjects, with the exception of Uriah, and burst out in tears of apology and say, "Uriah, I have sinned against you and my God. I did a terrible thing! I am full of unrighteousness! I am at fault! I have acted out of my flesh! I am so sorry! Please, please, please forgive me."

The halls of the palace would echo those words into eternity. But their voices would never be heard because David did just the opposite. Instead of walking in humility by confessing and asking Uriah for forgiveness, he stood even taller now in the flesh as he walked in pride and divisiveness.

You can almost hear the wheels of David's mind turning ten miles a minute as he begins to scheme, plot, and strategize. David thought of another strategy. He possibly said to himself, "Maybe if I invite him to dinner and get him drunk, maybe then he will go and sleep with his wife." But that did not work! Again, Uriah slept at the entrance of the palace with the other servants.

Warning! Warning! Send out the flares! Nothing is working for David. No amount of coaxing, nudging, pushing, or plain ol' saying, "Go home to your wife and make love to her..." could change the faithful and committed mindset Uriah had towards his duty of defending the Ark of God, Israel, and his fellow comrades in arms.

I will venture to say that David did not sleep that night. His thoughts were possibly overwhelmed with questions: What will others say once they find out? How will my concubines (ladies in waiting) view me now? Will the officers of the court lose respect for me and question my ability to rule? Will my children no longer trust their father's word as I have shown them that I am ruled by my emotions? ...

Such torture and unrest possibly permeated every hour of that night until David became exasperated. At his wits end, he devised a plan.

"This one should work..."

"Ooh, that's it!"

"...seems to be air tight..."

"God, I'm sorry but I have to do this..."

"I need to write a letter..."

"Okay, here goes..." he probably mumbled to himself.

Maybe the wastepaper basket and deerskin rug was strewn with papyrus paper from the many revisions David made to the letter. He possibly wrote the first line and felt the pangs of guilt shoot through the cavity of his abdomen. Maybe he sat back from the table and ran his hands through his hair at rapid speed to make sense of what he was about to do. The train of his robe probably dragged some of the paper along as he paced back and forth looking for a way out.

There was one, but he chose not to embrace it.

"It would cost me too much public pain. It would show me to be too weak, vulnerable, transparent..." he possibly thought to himself. But what great example it would have set for the subjects of his kingdom? What forceful blow it would have given to the enemy? And oh, what joy would have come to God's face to see a penitent heart!?

So David wrote. He wrote the letter which possibly sounded something like this,

> *"Most Honorable Captain Joab:*
>
> *I have been informed that the war is becoming more intense each day. Uriah has told me that you and the "Thirty" mighty men are holding the enemy at bay.*
>
> *Since Uriah has returned home, he has displeased me. He needs to be punished, but I do not wish to personally shed anymore blood. Captain Joab, do*

me this favor: Place Uriah on the front line of the battle. As the enemy approaches, you and the other men pull back without his knowledge so that he will be killed.

Make sure you send me a battle report on the outcome.

Your Royal Highness King David

Settled with his decision, David calls for Uriah the next morning and gives him the sealed letter to deliver to Captain Joab. Verses 16-17 and 24 of II Samuel 11 let us know that the enemy came up against Israel. Archers on the wall killed Uriah and other soldiers.

Upon hearing the news of Uriah and the other soldiers' death, David responded with what seemed to be a callous reply. Now, far be it from me to sit in judgment of this past great king. I love the man and I admire his tenacious spirit. But in reading the story again, I became upset. I felt that if I could, I would reach through the pages of time and smack the living day lights out of him. Disrespectful of me? Yes! But how could he?

Now, that was my flesh talking. I am calmed down now. I have since repented and am now reflective. But you know what? I want you to think about what he did, read his response then write me later and tell me what ran through your mind as you read it. Here is what David said, *"Well, tell Joab not to be discouraged; the sword kills one as well as another! Fight harder next time, and conquer the city!"* (LB).

Okay, am I the only one that felt a jolt of anger? I felt this way because I allowed myself to walk right into the story and become a part of it. Isn't that what we do sometimes? Isn't that why we can't seem to let go of the hurt someone else has inflicted on us. We go and relive the situation down to the minutest detail. I know we do it sometimes because

I've done it. I just did it a few moments ago and I was not the one that David injured.

There were several people who were emotionally and physically injured and/or killed as a result of this one act—lust being conceived: Uriah was killed, other soldiers lost their lives, Bathsheba mourned the lost of her husband along with the other wives who had lost their husbands and the mothers and fathers who had lost their sons, and the innocent child born out of David and Bathsheba's relationship died. The list could go on.

David had to endure the consequences of his actions. But most of all, I believe the rift in his relationship with God hurt him the most. Yes, he besought God for many days asking for Him to spare the child of his infidelity, but I truly believe it was the love relationship he had with the Father that affected him the most overall.

David's hurt, pain, and longing for forgiveness are evidenced by the deep, strong, riveting words of Psalm 51 which he wrote after he had defiled himself and Israel by sleeping with Bathsheba. He opens the chapter with this knee buckling, head down to the ground plea, *"Have mercy upon me, O God…blot out my transgression. Wash me thoroughly from mine iniquity, and cleanse me from my sin."*

First of all, David acknowledged his wrong-doing after being confronted by Nathan the prophet. He approaches God and throws himself on His altar of mercy. David was saying, "God, I know I am guilty and I don't deserve even a blink of attention from you, but, I need You to have mercy on me…"

I'm sure that from the previous talks David had with the Father, he understood that if mercy was extended he could get the opportunity to have an audience with God and plead the rest of his case. He could then ask to be washed thoroughly—through and through—not leaving any room for the stain of sin.

David knew that his actions separated him from his God. So he pleads with the Father, *"Cast me not away from thy presence; and take not thy holy spirit from me. Restore unto me the joy of thy salvation; and uphold me with thy free spirit."* He found himself alone without his Chief Companion, the One who was there when he defeated the bear and the lion that came after his sheep. He knew he would be defenseless against the pangs of guilt if he did not seek to restore his relationship with God.

This great king of Israel realized that a broken spirit, a repentant heart, an "I'm wrong, I'm guilty" attitude is what the Lord acknowledges. Pompousness, pride, and arrogance are abhorrent to Him. He should always be the greatest and highest seated One in every situation.

Okay, you may be saying, "The story of David is quite poignant and riveting, but I haven't wronged anyone like that!" You are correct! But, we must realize that big wrongs and small wrongs both require the same action—forgiveness. What David did was horrific. But what is greater than what David did is what God did for him. Yes, God forgave him.

Most assuredly God's forgiveness of David it is greater than the sin he committed *and* greater than any wrong you and I will ever do. "Why is that," you may ask? It is because of God's love for us. This love is unconditional and does not come with any risk factors or strings attached. That is why God extends forgiveness to us on a daily basis and allows His goodness and mercy to embrace us each day.

Now that we have a frame of reference, let's look at the word "forgiveness" again: cease to feel angry, pardon, remit, etc. As you can see, its definition is engulfed in action. It is a word that cannot accomplish anything on its own. It suggests that in order for it to become mobilized, someone or something must empower it. Forgiveness by itself cannot stand, for it requires someone to come be "fore" it to "give" it the juice it needs to accomplish its work.

Hence, you and I are ushered into the picture. We are now given the awesome opportunity to release salvation into the atmosphere and affect change on the part of all involved. Hallelujah, that's powerful!

In essence, when you and I stand in the position to forgive, we are elevated to the position of a king—a king who extends his scepter to the one he wants to enter his royal court. That scepter for you and I is forgiveness. When we extend forgiveness, we give permission for an individual to enter our court of compassion and mercy where a second chance, reconciliation with us, and healing awaits. Forgiveness stretches us to the point of love and reconciliation. It closes the gaps, it builds bridges, it fortifies foundations, it solidifies weak areas, and it empowers the one who extends it.

We now reside joyfully in the city of forgiveness. There is laughter, there is freedom, and there is singing. The atmosphere is light and clear, the presence of the Almighty God can be felt, and there is no line of demarcation separating us from each other.

What great liberty at such a wonderful cost!

REFLECTION ON LESSONS LEARNED

←*←*←*←*←*←*←

I have come to realize that whenever I ask God for something that is a part of His character, i.e., love, joy, faith, forgiveness, etc., I am saying in profound, earth-shaking terms, "God, I want more of You!" In addition, it is quite clear to me that I will, after asking, be faced with a situation that warrants that I exemplify and do the very thing I have asked Him to give me.

What are you trying to say, Hewlette? Well, let's say you are asking God for more love for people. How do you know if you are growing in that area? How do you know if He is answering your request? Let me tell you how you will know. God will often put some very unlikable persons in your path to test the very thing you desire. How you treat and respond to those individuals will be the litmus test to measure your success.

Is there something that you need and want from the Lord?

Is there a prayer request that has gone unanswered for some time now?

What do you think is holding up the process? No! Could it be?

Yes! It could be...

I have learned that forgiveness was the key to solving many of the issues I had. It brought healing to the deep-seated hurt and pain I was carrying. As a child, I was taught Matthew 6:9-13: "The Lord's Prayer." Repeating it over and over again did not teach me the reality and power of these words of assurance. Yes, I learned the prayer, but much of its accompaniment (actions) was so far behind me that the future seemed closer. Living out certain aspects of the prayer in my life was another thing.

Verse 12 says, "*And forgive us our debts* (wrongs), *as we forgive our debtors* (those who wronged us)." This sounds to me that there is a contingency factor for me receiving the best from the Lord. I can only be forgiven *when* I forgive others. I can only have access to His presence *once* I have done what is required. I can only walk in authority *when* I have submitted to the will of God—forgiving others.

I also learned that when I extend forgiveness to others, I am sitting in the highest seat available at the time—in heavenly places with Christ Jesus. There is fullness of joy there. There is solitude, contentment, satisfaction, and great peace in His presence. So you see forgiveness benefits us more than we could imagine.

Love, mercy, and humility are wonderful bedfellows of forgiveness. You cannot forgive without extending these attributes. So go ahead and do it! Take the risk and walk away knowing that all heaven is standing with you.

Begin to breathe again, to see clearly, to walk in liberty, to sing again, to...

CHAPTER EIGHT

THE PAIN OF PRAISE

*"Just when the caterpillar thought the world
was over, it became a butterfly."*
—Anonymous

Time. What is time? Is it the numbers on a clock that
are illuminated by the second, minute, and hour hands?
No, time is much, much deeper than that. Time embraces
you, it shifts you, it tugs at your heart, and it just doesn't
make sense sometimes. Time would seem to have a mind of
its own, caring nothing about our perspective on whatever
"time" it is.

But time is time: a working, shifting, moving, doing
"thing" that exists outside of eternity. It has its limits, but
appears at time to have none. Whenever the time of much
joy and happiness begin to flee we sigh, "Why does it have
to end?" But when the time of trouble and pain comes we
ask, "When will it all end?"

King Solomon thought about this "thing" called time and
found that...

*To every thing there is a season, and a time to every
purpose under the heaven: A time to be born, and a*

time to die; a time to plant, and a time to pluck up that which is planted; A time to kill, and a time to heal; a time to break down, and a time to build up; a time to weep, and a time to laugh; a time to mourn, and a time to dance; a time to cast away stones, and a time to gather stones together; a time to embrace, and a time to refrain from embracing; a time to get, and a time to lose; a time to keep, and a time to cast away; a time to rend, and a time to sew; a time to keep silence, and a time to speak; a time to love, and a time to hate; a time of war, and a time of peace (Ecclesiastes 3:1-8).

Now that's time! It is a season in our life that is marked by situations that are defined by what we experience — joys, disappointments, losses, gains, setbacks, advances, etc. A clock would not be able to contain the "times" of experiences we have encountered, but we can tell the times of our lives by where we are now in comparison to where we were.

Now what does time have to do with "The Pain of Praise?" Everything! Every minute detail of our life exists on two things: thankfulness and complaint. Just two categories, that's all. No third, fourth, or fifth column needed. It's either or... There are no gray areas, even if we allowed our minds to wonder the corridor of our intellect.

Why do I say this? Well, I Thessalonians 5:18 says, *"In every thing give thanks: for this is the will of God in Christ Jesus concerning you."* Note the first word... "**In**." He did not say thank Him for everything. No. On the contrary, for if we were to do that, there would be a long line of concerned, loving, and faithful people knocking down the doors of the nearest mental institution. Of course we would not be checking ourselves in, but our relative, friend, husband, wife, etc. would rush to the obvious conclusion that we are crazy and check us in.

Can you imagine saying, "Lord, I just thank and praise You that I was in a car accident where I lost my left eye and right foot?" Or... "I just honor You, Father, for letting my house burn down where I lost everything that was so precious to me?" Or better still... "Glory be to Your awesome, brilliant name for letting me get cancer and now I only have six months to live?"

Of course we would not say that! But we see a burst of energy, celebration, and hope from the "In" of that scripture. It ("**In** everything give thanks...") is loaded with expectation and closure, for it gives us a sneak preview and suggests (or hints) that there is an end, an out, and a favorable outcome.

No matter what is happening, no matter what situation is facing us, no matter the problem, praise is comely and appropriate for the time. While we are experiencing hurt God is saying, "Praise Me **in** it." Once you praise "**in**" the situation, God makes Himself visible **in** the middle of it. Visible to the point where others get to see your God defend, comfort, and protect you in the midst of the storm, in the midst of pain, in the midst of the fire.

The Old Testament story of the three Hebrew boys (Daniel 3) is a clear, profound, and moving picture of one's commitment to Jehovah and Jehovah's commitment to His people. Imagine making up your mind that you will not praise or pay homage to another god even if it costs you your life. There must have been some wrestling of the will to go through the physical act of such a conscious decision.

Here you are with hands bound, facing the fury of a prominent king, hearing the crackling of wood in the fire, and absorbing the heat of an oven that was set seven times hotter than its normal temperature. Do you have a choice in the matter? Can you change your mind this late in the story of your life?

"Run! Hide! Beg for mercy! Give in! Bow!" I can hear the taunting of the adversary as the Hebrew boys faced their fiery future. But what a bright and revelatory future it would be—a future that would still read as current as today's newspaper headline, a future that would be the stable foundation from which others would stand, and a future that would be the measuring stick and barometer for the conviction and commitment of others.

Their determination to stand for the principles of God no matter what the cost brought a great king and nation to its knees. The fourth man, the Son of the living God, rose from His seat at the right hand of power and stood in the midst of the flames with His three sons. What great honor! What great privilege! What an awesome move of God!

Can you, for a moment, imagine yourself passing through time into eternity? As you approach the magnificence of God's presence, you peek through the clouds just in time to see Jesus sitting in anticipation. Waiting eagerly, He peeks over glory's sphere and watches the Babylonian guards put themselves in position to throw the Hebrew boys into the fire.

You view the events of eternity while staring back at the trials of time. There's a rush of emotions as you are overcome by the sure exuberance and awe-inspiring outcome. It's almost as if you wish you could run back to the Hebrew boys to let them know everything is going to be all right, just hold on. But suddenly something uncommon, too marvelous for words happens—the Father nudges the Son and says,

"Yes, it's time, Son. It's time to stand in the fire with My sons."

You jump. You cheer. You say,

"Yes! Yes! I knew it! I knew it! Jesus is on the way!"

What a great sight that must have been when Jesus appeared into the fire with the Hebrew boys? Could they have predicted a better outcome? Did their minds dare to try and grasp the endless love and care God had for them? This we do know: the king and his subjects now knew to what lengths Jehovah God would go to deliver His people. They met the God of the universe through the Hebrew boys' act of praise—total commitment.

Their level of commitment showed the greatest praise the Hebrew boys could ever give to the Father. Their act of worship was birthed out of their pain. It is safe to assume that they endured ridicule, name-calling, threats, and shame. Of the thousands of people who bowed their knees at the sound of the Babylonian music, these three brave soldiers of Jehovah stood tall in the presence of God and His holy angels.

Saints of the 21st century know that praising God during the "bad" times is not easy. It goes against the will, it pushes against the tide of our reality, it works its way through the cobwebs of our mind, and it shifts us to a place of questions. It then becomes a sacrifice—a sacrifice that at times does not make sense.

Why should I be thankful when everything around me is going wrong? Where is the God I love when my best friend has hurt me beyond repair? What is wrong with my being silent and unresponsive to God because my wife has cheated on me? Why should I lift my hands and worship when I can't face my family because of my past?

The why's, how's, where's, who's, and what's of our lives can strain out the voice of God. They sometimes bleed us so dry that the little praise we have left is carefully boxed up for fear of crumbling. Habakkuk understood this, but he had a solution to a petrifying problem:

"Even though the fig trees have no blossoms, and there are no grapes on the vine; even though the olive crop fails, and the fields lie empty and barren; even though the flocks die in the fields, and the cattle barns are empty, yet I will rejoice in the Lord! I will be joyful in the God of my salvation" (Habakkuk 3:17-18, LB).

Rejoice! Rejoice! Rejoice!

A cursory reading of this scripture would make it hard for us to fathom that someone could muster up enough energy to part their lips and say, "Thank You, Lord," when <u>everything</u> has been wiped out—no money, no food, no car, no bank account to fall back on, no roof over the head, nothing growing from the ground, no thing—zilch—yet still, have a healthy perspective on life.

But when we look closely at the scripture, we find that a key ingredient was overlooked: *"I will rejoice **in the Lord**! I will be joyful **in the God of my salvation.**"* The **"in's"** of this scripture are key to keeping us focused in the days of adversity. This prepositional phrase is backed up by and packed with two very powerful nouns—Lord and God.

The nouns are defined within themselves as they speak of one that is high, omnipotent, in control, in charge, and all sufficient. Thus the pain of failure is diffused at the acknowledgement and acceptance of Whom we joy in—the God of our salvation... The God of our rescue... The God of our retribution... The God of repossession and restoration... The God of "double for your trouble"... The God of turning nothing into something... The God who is the Creator creating..."

Please know that trouble and pain will come. But what we do (rejoice or complain) during these times will signal whether we understand who we truly are in Christ and whose we are.

Let me share a little story with you that I experienced one summer. My younger brother, Daniel, and I were sitting on our parents' porch one warm summer evening talking about the meaning of some of the Jamaican proverbs we sometimes hear our parents use to enlighten our sometimes-colorless imagination. The sun was setting and the sky had a beautiful orange hue that seemed to rest on the tops of the clouds.

As I viewed the sunset, I looked towards one of the marble granite pillars of the porch and beheld an awesome sight. A spider had begun to weave a web. I did not see the markings of the web at first; I just saw this small creature moving from north to east, to the south, and then to the west. I marveled because it seemed as if it was moving about in thin air, guided by an invisible hand with such freedom and confidence.

My brother and I watched in amazement as it weaved up and down, across, diagonal... What a great artistic design this little creature of insignificance and need was forming. All this was done, it seemed, without any fear of disruption or attack from a predator.

Darkness began to fall, and as we continued our conversation, we occasionally glanced over towards the pillar to behold the sight.

"Why is he building such a large web," I asked my brother?

"To catch as many insects he can get," he responded.

We marveled at the great wisdom that God had instilled in this little creature. We even exchanged stories of encounters with spider webs in unlikely places.

Have you ever walked up into a spider web? Well, my brother and I have. We both agree that it is one awful thing to get off your face and clothes. It seems the spiders' webs are an invisible silk thread of adhesive.

The next morning I dashed down the stairs to see what became of the mighty structure "Mr. Spider" was building. As I peered toward the sun-strewn sky, I realized that the spider had weaved an approximate twenty by twenty-four inch web. It used the strength of a nail that protruded from the pillar, the top of the tallest flower, and the edge of the flower box to build its maze of astonishment and great fortitude.

As I inspected this awesome piece of artwork, I noticed some glitches and spaces. There were little bundles deposited at different areas on this maze; I moved in closer for a careful inspection. I realized that the spider had not only protected himself, but he had also caught many predators in his web. Even more astonishing was the fact that the web was started as darkness began to fall; however, it was completed in darkness.

This darkness allowed the spider to rest in unwavering hope that there would be an even larger catch by the first light of morning. Its offense lit up the space that was not visible to the naked eye, but proved an immeasurable compensation for an auspicious work done.

As I stood in total shock, I began to think of the possible motives of "Mr. Spider" when he first set off to build this web. Watching the weaving of the web revealed that this spider had begun to strategize. His intent was to protect himself, to insulate himself from any possible harm, and to catch the enemy when it least expected it. He made plans for an offensive attack. His tireless weaving at dusk prophesied a glorious and victorious morning.

In many ways, our praise and worship of God mirrors the workings of the spider. It is likely that the spider is aware of its web's frailty when it comes to human tendencies, i.e., wiping it away during cleaning, running into it on our way to work, and cutting part of its design while clipping the tops of the bushes. Here he faces something far greater in size and wisdom, something much greater than he—humans, but he still builds.

He constructed this awesome, yet powerful design as it began to get dark, setting up his defensive attack. We too set up our defenses: as it begins to get dark; as we begin to feel the pain of discouragement, the pain of adversity, the sharp jagged edge of the knife of betrayal; as we begin to be overwhelmed by the sorrows of death; as we strain to lift our heads from the agony of sudden defeat; and as we struggle to stretch the ends of our finances so they can somehow meet.

Yes, we spin our own web of praise in the shadow of darkness. We spin our web of offense and defense in the lonely times in our lives. We praise in the face of danger. We glorify God in the depths of despair. We shout, "Hallelujah!" with the guilt of hurting someone we love. And we bow our knees and become prostrate before the God of the universe while clutching the struggles of day-to-day life. But we continue to spin! Spin the web of praise.

What a great sight we begin to behold as the first sparkle of light appears? What awesome sight of beauty and strength we embrace as God reveals to us the failed plots and tricks of the enemy as they are caught in the web of our praise! What great groaning of pain we hear as the enemy of our soul limps from before the presence of God after coming to accuse us before the Lord! What a terrific sight to witness when those who ridiculed and talked against us are caught standing with their mouths ajar, amazed at the mighty hand of God in our life!

Yes! Our praise in the time of pain proves that we were selected for something more wonderful than just being churchgoers. It shatters the careless belief of the outside world that we are just talkers, not doers. And it empowers us to unveil the divine desire and will of our Father regarding our lives.

Praise Him in the good times! Praise Him in the bad times! Praise Him all the time!

The end of Hosea 14:2 says, *"...So will we render the calves of our lips."* This is a simple, yet profound verse which basically says, "We will offer the sacrifice of praise;" that which is costly is a struggle to get out, but it must be done. It is a praise that is formed out of difficult situations and becomes a divinely orchestrated dart through the heart of the enemy.

Let our praise be one that is birthed out of our knowledge of Him rather than our worrying about our situation.

We must fight for our right to worship the Highest. We must peel away the fears and discouragement from before our eyes and receive the revelation of His love to us. In doing so, we will have gained a fantastic advantage over the enemy as our attention is focused on the right thing—the praise and worship of the Most High God.

Situations come to pull us down in the dumps of oppression and depression. Shifting to praise lifts our head and gives us confidence in the providential hand of God. It catapults us into the realm of eternity where we can see the end from the beginning. Praise helps us to declare the omnipotence of God and brings into captivity the very thoughts that tried to enslave us in the negative corridors of our mind.

The need to speak aloud what God has given us sometimes is necessary to get our minds in check and to quench the fiery darts that the enemy tries to use against us. See it! Declare it! Move forward with confidence and determination!

I have a "little boyfriend" that has taught me a great lesson. He was only 18 months at the time when he said something that truly recapitulates this entire chapter. Whenever he has a toy, food, or something that he enjoys holding, from a distance you can hear him saying, "Mine! Mine! Mine!" Now mind you, no one has come up to him and asked him for that thing yet. But with the slightest sound of another person's approach, he begins to announce, "Mine! Mine! Mine!"

Now you may ask, "How does that sum up this chapter?" Thanks for asking.

What do we have that the enemy seems to be attacking? What is so dear and near to us that the least sign of disruption causes us to panic and doubt the promises of God? Well, my little friend has proven to us at such a young age that announcing our resolve creates a barrier of protection. It sets up weapons for an offensive attack and reassures us of God's promises.

Our praise to the Lord sends a devastating blow to the enemy. Our shout says to satan—

"Mine! Get your filthy hands off."

"Mine! The will of God shall prevail."

"Mine! I am committed to God to the end."

Mine! My life belongs to Jehovah, not you."

Mine! I am a victor not a victim."

Think about it and speak it! The praise of our God makes a difference in every aspect of our lives. Our sanity depends on it, our destiny is tied up with it, our prosperity lives for it, and the hearts and lives we will reach are waiting for it.

Yes, talking aloud is our way of seeing and declaring what God has ordained for our lives. The enemy is the prince of the power of the air. So let's open up our mouths and send those power-packed missiles straight into the enemy's camp. Let's listen for the explosion in our praise. Sleep without worrying about tomorrow. Know that a brighter day is just a few hours away. And let's leap for joy for the glory of the Lord is here!

REFLECTION ON LESSONS LEARNED

←–*←–*←–*←–*←–*←–*←

I don't have all the answers to say, "Do this, do that…" But know that what I share with you here is based upon my own experiences and what I have gleaned from reading God's Word.

Praises do what no physical weapon could ever accomplish. Of course we know that *the weapons of our warfare are not carnal, but mighty through God to the pulling down of strong holds* (II Corinthians 4:10). Our praises sets up an ambush against the enemy, for they are strategically and divinely activated weapons that destroy his plans and schemes.

Here's what I do when I find myself in a crisis:

- I begin to worship God with the pain.
- Other times whenever the enemy comes with bad news and I feel the urge to cry, guess what I do? I cry for a few seconds sometimes and I tell the Lord, "Ouch, that hurts." Then I get up, refocus my mind, and begin to sing a love song to the Lord. Before long, I am transported into His presence and He heals the wound and calms my spirit.
- Other times, I put on praise and worship compact disks and listen and sing along to songs that minister to my spirit. This helps to put my mind on good things. Paul encouraged us in Philippians 4:8,

> *"Finally, brethren, whatever is true, whatever is honorable, whatever is right, whatever is pure, whatever is lovely, whatever is of good repute, if there is any excellence and if anything worthy of praise, dwell on these things"* (NASB).

Because it is through our spirit that the Holy Spirit communicates (Spirit to spirit), it is often the place the enemy tries to attack by creating chaos, problems, and heartache in and around us. This verse in Philippians tells us to fill our thoughts with good things. It is so that our spirit will not become tainted and filthy with ungodly and irreverent thoughts. We create an unholy ground for the presence of God when we linger in the mire of hopelessness, doubt, pessimism, and anger, just to name a few.

Here's a good lesson I learned and am ever learning—because I have suffered so much hurt in the past and have inflicted some on others myself, I take a quiet moment and think about what lessons God is trying to teach me in all of this.

- I begin to think about how much that person must be hurting to contrive evil against me.
- I then begin to intercede on behalf of the one who hurt me; before long, the Holy Spirit comes and places in me a heart of sympathy towards that individual.
- Another thing I rush to do is to forgive quickly because it closes whatever gap the enemy had devised to bring separation and enmity.

Now mind you, forgiveness does not mean the wrong is erased totally from your mind. No! However, forgiveness allows the healing process to begin immediately; it allows our minds to be pure towards those who may have wronged us. So in essence what I am saying is that forgiveness can be instant; it is the healing that may take some time.

If our focus remains on what truly matters, then we will not give the enemy any foothold in the relationship and/or situation.

- Praising God creates the air that is needed to help the wound heal faster than expected.
- Worship keeps the band-aid of self-pity and "woe is me syndrome" from covering areas that need to be exposed for healing.
- Praise and worship helps to shift us to a position of power and authority, for the ground we stand on is wholly/entirely occupied by God's presence.

Whenever anything goes wrong, I try to practice the following:

- I speak to the situation and declare an expected end.
- I learn to ask God to give me spiritual strategies to fight whatever the enemy brings my way.
- I trust God for my well-being, therefore, I leave every situation in His hand, for He has empowered me to fight and not sit down and let the enemy run havoc of my life.

- I learned that the pain is temporal, but His glory is eternal, consistent, and ready to rise up in me, in agreement with my faith, every time.

CHAPTER NINE

VALLEY LOW

*"I know God won't give me anything I can't handle,
I just wish He didn't trust me so much."*
— Mother Teresa

Just when I thought nothing else could go wrong... The moment things had started to become clear... Just when I thought I was reaching the zenith of my experience ... The instance I started to experience God in a supernatural way... Right when I thought I had a new perspective on the road ahead... Just when I could see hope peering its eyes through the darkened clouds, I lay wondering, "What am I doing here, again?'

It was a cold Sunday morning in January when I was awakened with a severe throbbing pain in my upper left leg. As a matter of fact, it was my birthday and my friend June had come over to celebrate it with me. We took a look at my leg, but saw no signs of swelling or bruising. After some poking and rubbing, I decided that I would not let it stand in the way of my birthday plans.

We traveled to Fairfax, Virginia where an anxious cat awaited food and change of litter. My boss was out of town and I was her trusted house-sitter. After taking care of the cat's needs, June and I decided to go to my favorite sushi restaurant to have brunch. As we began to satisfy our hunger, a severe pain shot through my left leg and up my hip. It became so unbearable that we ended the brunch earlier than expected and returned to my boss's house.

"Your leg is swollen, Hewlette!" June shouted as we entered the brightly lit kitchen. It was quite obvious in the loosely fitting blue jeans I was wearing. The swelling was visible from my calve muscle to my toes. Immediately another pain shot through my leg and I hobbled to the couch to sit and prop my leg up. We both were pretty scared, as we did not know what it was, and we wrestled with the thought of calling the ambulance.

As the evening wore on, the swelling went down. The pain was still there, but it was bearable. We watched a few movies and wished it would snow hard enough that we would not have to go to school the next day—Monday morning. Well, we got our wish. The snow fell and brought ice with it. Schools were canceled and the streets were silent.

June left that morning after making sure the swelling had gone down. I told her I would be fine and that I may have injured myself by doing too much cheering and gyration at the church basketball tournament on Saturday night. I thought of all the likely possibilities that would cause such pain and swelling and could find no other than the Saturday night activities. Furthermore, I did not need anything else to go wrong in my life, as it was just the first anniversary of the surgery to remove a large tumor from my abdomen.

By Monday afternoon the leg began to swell again. I propped it up and began massaging it for comfort. In my heart I was praying, "God, please move this thing... Please move whatever is causing the pain and swelling..."

By Wednesday, I was dragging the leg wherever I walked. It felt like dead weight on my body. The swelling had gone down, but the pain came and went. It was like it had a mind of its own.

As I lay in bed Wednesday night, I propped my legs up on three pillows and prayed for God to send relief. I felt that this was a direct attack by the devil on my body. I had been exercising, eating the right foods, and taking my vitamins as the doctors had instructed. For the entire year, I had frequent checkups, followed strict health guidelines, and did what I needed to do for the best interest of my body.

Thursday morning came and we had delayed opening. Seeing I was so close to the school where I taught, I took my time in getting dress. I noticed the swelling had gone down some, and the pain had subsided.

By mid afternoon, one of my colleagues noticed that my left leg was swollen. I rehearsed the story of what I had endured for the past few days. She became very troubled and said,

"I wonder if you have a blood clot in your leg." I stood as if in a trance. I remembered that every time I asked God to move the thing that was causing the pain I heard the voice say,

"You have a blood clot."

Of course at that announcement I became irate and told the devil,

"You're a liar! I am healed."

"Hewlette, what if it's a blood clot," she said?

"I'm going to the emergency room now!" I responded.

I was given identification number 033191091 and was told I had to wait until a bed became available. The inside of the emergency room corridor looked like a newly opened sardine can. Patients were everywhere, against the walls, near the elevators, and by the nurses' station. If there was an opening, it was quickly filled with another gurney.
It resembled a scene from the television show M*A*S*H.
Gurneys lined the emergency hallway and the nurses mean-

dered their way through the traffic taking blood pressures and drawing blood from one vein to the next. If you had an arm, you became a victim of the sharp piercing needles and oxygenated vials.

I felt a shift of my bed and looked up. It was a nurse getting ready to wheel me to the ex-ray and imaging ward. As I approached the entrance of the corridor, an eerie feeling came over me. I had been here just eleven months prior. What was I doing here again?

There were other patients ahead of me, so I was left on the gurney waiting my turn. I sat up to peer down the opposite hallway, but a patient who sat motionless in a wheelchair blocked my view. Her arms and face had gauze and tubes flowing from various points; I struggled to say something to her. We both looked at each other and broke the silence with a tight, yet defined smile.

"Lord, is this why I am here," I asked God in my mind?

Without an answer I heard the woman say,

"Hello."

Out of the shock of embarrassment, I mumbled,

"Hello."

I asked her if she were okay and had anyone come to see her. Her answer melted my heart and I no longer worried about my condition, but became very concerned about her.

"I don't have anyone to visit" she exclaimed.

"My mother and sister live in another part of town… My mother is in the hospital and my sister needs help to get around," she shared.

I immediately began to pray for her in the Spirit. I tried to maneuver the bed to get a little closer so I could touch her, but the nurse came out and began pushing me into the imaging room.

The entire time the nurse was pouring warm gel on my leg and pushing the instrument up and down into the back of my leg, my thoughts were centered on that woman. I resumed interceding for her and hoped that when I was released from the imaging room, she would still be in the hallway. I was sorely disappointed to find that she was not there.

The results of the sonogram came back—a blood clot behind the knee.

"We will have to keep you for about four to five days for observation and for as much dissolution of the clot as possible," the doctor informed me.

Those were not words I wanted to hear. I was through with being a patient in the hospital. One time was enough!

Do you believe God has a sense of humor? Well, I do. He must have a sense of humor to deal with some of the antics we perform. Antics that we even have the audacity to do during prayer—telling him what to do and when to do it. You may be wondering why I raise this question, but I have my reasons. Here it is.

Remember that whenever I felt the pain in my leg, I asked God to move whatever was causing it? Well, I may have brought a smile of compassion to His face. If He had allowed it (the blood clot) to dislodge, you would not be reading my story, and I would not have gotten the opportunity to pen these words. According to the doctor, if any part of the clot had broken off, it would have traveled straight to my lungs, then my heart, and then sudden death.

"Many people don't survive with a clot as long as you did... you are lucky to be alive," he expressed.

Of course you and I know that luck had nothing to do with it. My Father in heaven and His angels were keeping guard over me even in my ignorance.

I am made stronger by every negative situation that has affected my life. Yes, sickness and disappointment have come, but they were turned into something positive that brought the ultimate glory to God. That is the great beauty it has brought about in me.

His glory is revealed through my will and determination to stay focused on His desire for my life. And His glory is revealed in my whispering a prayer for that lonely soul in the hospital corridor. His glory is revealed through my testimony of triumphant victory over the clamoring claws of death that swung to grip me. And His glory is being revealed even now as your eyes pan left to right at the speed of at millimeter of a second, to absorb, regurgitate, and ingest the goodness of God on these pages.

REFLECTION ON LESSONS LEARNED

←*←*←*←*←*←*←

Through this experience, I have found that the pain and disappoint the enemy causes can never block out the light of Jesus' love, for He crushes the darkness with the very light of His presence. Like the sun, God's love is always there to bring needed nutrients to sustain us in the times of storms, difficulties, and setbacks.

Praise the Lord! God has designed, especially for me, light along the way. Sometimes it is shining so full like a bright Summer's day; at other times, I may have to move back the furniture and curtains just to see a ray. But through it all, I know that the light is always there, shining and being the warmth in the middle of a cold and gloomy day. Praise the Lord!

satan (intentional lower case usage), on the other hand, is a non-entity. Yes, he is a force to fight offensively and defensively, but his power and existence are limited to the amount of rope God gives him to stretch his ugly neck over the fence of my liberty.

Right now, satan is in a holding cell—earth's atmosphere—and he is only given limited power. As a result, he walks around roaring like a lion to scare the ones he can into thinking that he's greater than he really is.

But there is something much more profound we need to learn and embrace. You and I have been given **all** power over **all** the power of satan, *"Behold, I give unto you power...over all the power of the enemy..."* (Luke 10:19). We just simply do not know we have it or we choose not to exercise it. My sister Julianne once said to me, "It's a tragedy when the enemy knows your potential and you do not."

When we are at those valley times, the enemy shows up like a big bully to growl and scare us into thinking he has the upper hand. But I tell you one thing, if you can begin to realize who you are in Christ and get just enough energy to stand up to him, you will see satan run like a coward in the face of a foe—you.

satan is afraid of your faith; he trembles at your confidence; he shrieks at the very thought of your thinking you are victorious. There is no place for him there. He feeds off defeat, he thrives in fear, he relishes doubt, and he gains control in lost identities.

Try speaking God's word to your situation then watch how your faith and confidence grow and your perception change towards the situation. Mine did and I learned that my words are weapons of warfare that terrorize the enemy.

Begin to see and sense the change. See your situation turning out for the good because you love the Lord. Declare your end from the beginning. Don't wait for things to change. Speak the change and before long, you will find yourself experiencing it.

You are now sitting in heavenly places with Christ Jesus. You have been elevated to positions of great power and influence. Walk in it! Trust the God in you to do more than you could ever imagine.

No, he does not have permission to beat me up! No, you and I are not open season for the enemy! No, he cannot just walk all over us and go about his business. He may try to attack our bodies in order to disrupt our spirit (mind) to affect negative influence over our soul. But thanks be to God. Christ steps in and lifts up a standard against him, for only Christ has ownership over our souls.

So, like Job we can say, *"And though after my skin worms destroys this body, yet in my flesh shall I see God"* (Job 19:26) We're going to come out of this (sickness and disease) 'cause He's excited our soul to get our spirit in check so that our body can become alive again.

Gloooory!!!

CHAPTER TEN

A TEST TO TEST ME: THE JOLT

*"Struggles are like rungs in a ladder leading you to the top.
For you to get there, you must hold on as you
climb to the next level."*
—H.A. Pearson

Years had passed since I was fired from the private investigative firm. I received my graduate degree in education; my future looked mighty fine. As with many things that have transpired in my life, I have come to see that not until the ultimate call has been answered will there be peace.

The news finally came. Months of studying, meeting with tutors, praying and fasting, wishing and hoping, and trying to see down the road of my future would quietly come to rest on my kitchen table. All that energy over the months oozed out of me to prove one thing—I am a failure? For a brief moment I thought so.

I was hired by the Fairfax County Public School system as an English teacher one year before I graduated from Johns Hopkins University's School of Business and Education. Having never taught before, I was quite surprised that the Principal of the school offered me the position with no professional experience. It was as if the job came looking for me.

I had worked at this job now for over four years, and I knew beyond a shadow of a doubt that I was destined to be there to move on to greater things in my educational pursuits. If it were my time to leave, I felt that God would have to express this Himself to me. I really don't ask for much, most of the time, but felt that as He had provided this job for me so miraculously, I knew He would make things work out in my favor.

I made my way down to the kitchen to have dinner that evening and behold, the envelope reared its lily-white head from between the other brown, yellow, and blue envelopes that signaled that "William" had written me again. I mean "Bill" (unwanted bills and junk mail). The other envelopes containing bills looked more inviting than the lily-white one, so I ventured to rifle through those first. I knew I could no longer avoid opening it, so I stretched forth my hand, with no great urgency, picked up the envelope, and slowly ripped it open.

"Uh-oh" I said aloud as I removed its content.

"Don't worry, you did just fine!" my Dad exclaimed.

"I'm sure it's okay," he reassured me.

I heard him. But then again I did not, as I was so focused on what my eyes shouted back to my brain—

"You didn't pass!"

Tears began to fill my eyes and I fought hard not to let any of it waste onto the paper I held in my hands. Why should I cry? This has to be a huge mistake. There is no way on earth I've failed at the thing I do best.

"Maybe I'm being tested to see how I would respond under pressure," I convinced myself.

Not trusting my eyes alone, I maneuvered my body toward "my spot" at the kitchen table and slowly pulled out the chair. With a quiet breath of resignation, I plopped myself down and held my head in my hands in disbelief.

"It's gonna be okay. We prayed already and we believe for the best" my Mom chimed.

I heard her, but then again, I didn't. How could they say such words to me? Do they really even know what is at stake here? Can they, even with a little stretch of the imagination, conjure up the unsavory feelings that began to flow through my dazed body? For that moment, I did not believe they could.

An eerie silence hovered in that warm friendly kitchen. I could hear nothing but my heart beating—beating as if someone was pounding his or her fist against a wooden door. The thumps echoed in my mind. Suddenly I realized that I was in a world all by myself.

After a few seconds of silence, I raised my torso up from its slumped position, grabbed a pen, and began writing the scores down to calculate them for myself. Surely this was sent to me in error. I did well! I could feel it, but then again, I didn't. It was if I was slipping in and out of reality.

I had been here once before and the feeling was heart wrenching. Prior to graduating from Johns Hopkins University in Baltimore, Maryland, I had to take the National Teachers Examination. I received the test scores of the exam. They arrived during my absence.

That Summer I had decided to treat myself to a wonderful vacation. I stayed away from home the entire school break. I remember my mother calling me by telephone to alert me that the scores were back.

"Do you want me to open it and read it to you?" she asked.

I saw no fireworks lighting up the skies and heard no band playing the tune to "Pomp and Circumstances"—all signaling a terrific outcome—graduation. I just did not feel that envelope had good news in it.

"No way!" I exclaimed.

"I'm scared… What if it ruins my vacation?" I chimed.

During the interim and prior to my return home, another copy of the examination came. I wrestled with the thought,

"Why did I receive the second one? Which one was I to venture opening first?"

I opened the copy I received last and a big grin spread across my face. I quickly opened the other and immediately, my joy turned to consternation.

"What in the world is going on here? How am I supposed to figure this out?" I quipped.

On the first test result a big, bright, bolded word shouted the outcome—"Failed!" My successful matriculation through graduate school hinged on this one document. Without it, an aspiring teacher could not grace the podium with his or her presence while walking to the beat of "Pomp and Circumstances." I knew the urgency of the hour and needed to know where I stood.

Sitting back and taking a deep breath, I reviewed the examinations and found that the first copy was sent to me in error. They had miscalculated and sent me the wrong scores. What a "Hallelujah" time that was for me!

Could it be that this was dé ja vu all over again?

"Lord, whatever Your will is for my life, I know that you will make it plain," I said to myself.

Did I truly believe it or was I creating insulation to guard me against what I regretted. Using my forefinger to trace the numbers across the column, I slowly read them aloud, "178, 182, and 170." By reading them aloud it seemed that I had convinced myself that I had made it by the skin of my teeth. I needed a 532 to be a bona fide, licensed professional. Not qualified, but bona fide. Qualified, I am. Or so I thought.

Math has never been my strong suit, so I did not want to just rely on calculating the scores in my head. I began to write them down slowly as I fought back the tears that sat at the threshold of my eyelids. Daring me to blink caused a deluge of emotions to come pouring out of body. I raised my eyebrows, spread my eyes wide-open, and defied my tears the luxury of a flow. I added the first column.

"Mmmm...Ah-man...Gosh...Oh No, not me!" came pouring from my lips with despair.

I could feel the blood vessels in my eyes begin to crowd my faced as if they were anxiously waiting for some great convention to take place. My mind began to anticipate the barrage of questions that would come flying at me,

"What's the score?"

"How'd you do?"

"Did you pass?"

I heard them, but then again, I didn't. It was as if I was standing alone in a cold lonely place, asking questions but hearing my voice echo the answer back instead.

While staring off into space, I muttered,

"Can't try anymore. Time is up for me. This is it. There are no more chances."

A thick silence suddenly permeated the room again. It felt as if my parents were now draped in the shroud of pain that embraced me when I first saw the scores.

With visible disappointment over their faces, yet trying to say words of comfort, my Mom looked at me and said,

"If we pay for it, can you take it again?"

"Did she not hear me the first time?" I shouted in my mind.

"Mom, I told you... This is it! No more tests."

Maybe she's just in denial or maybe she believes in miracles.

"Why would she disturb the agony I was feeling with some empty ray of hope," I thought.

I felt that I needed to get up and go. Go somewhere! Go anywhere! I would speak to no one, not even God! And no one better dare speak to me!

I knew the feelings that now began to darken my vision into the future were not healthy ones. The enemy began to send his vicious venomous words to wound me at the core of my reality—my faith and trust in God. My emotions ran up and down, sideways, and in a circle. I felt like one big ball of nothingness.

"What was I good for? I can't even pass a lousy exam," I began to mutter to myself.

Excusing myself from the presence of my parents, I ascended the stairs to my room with great urgency. It was as if I had company waiting for me. As I walked alongside the bed to the cherry-wood framed mirror, I stood looking at my face. Into my eyes I peered as if waiting for an answer.

The blood rushed again to my face and the tears poured like water from an overflowed fountain. My body just could not hold up to the anguish that crammed every nerve cell inside my somewhat oversized frame. It was as if I turned into a child all over again—needing attention, a soft gentle word of assurance, or a bear hug that would somehow take the pain, the agony of defeat, the embarrassment, the let down, the disappoint... all away.

But that did not happen. I strained to see my reflection as my eyes began to burn from the tears. A headache ensued and all I could see myself doing is crawling up in a corner and rocking myself to sleep. I began to question myself. I knew deep down that there must be an answer, some small light at the end of this torturous tunnel...

"Why? Why now? Why me?"

There was a definite struggle taking place here, for as I wrestled with the thoughts of failure, I found my spirit fighting back. As the tears rolled down my cheek, I writhed in disappointment and heard these words flow from my lips,

"I'll still trust You no matter what."

"I'll still do what you want me to do!"

The pain intensified and the pangs of hurt seemed to have a louder voice than the loving inner voice that rushed in to support my battered emotional state.

Peering beyond the image of my face in the mirror, as if looking for a nobler reflection, I again asked,

"Why? Why is this happening to me?"

Although I asked the question, deep inside of me, I knew the answer. The answer that was there from the time I told God that I knew He loved me and had my best interest at heart. How long have I known the answer? For over nine years now.

Trusting God for necessities in life has never been an overwhelming problem for me. Through the many obstacles, disappointments, and occasional mix-ups, I have had to rely on who He is rather than on where I was. I have found God to be my personal physician, my Defender among friends and foes, my Provider, and Best Friend.

"Haven't I learned the lesson yet?" I thought so and assumed this only to be a devastating blow to my pride, my future, and my livelihood. Can I leave my school quietly? I don't know. Or do I?

CHAPTER ELEVEN

A TEST TO TEST ME:
THE ROLLER COASTER RIDE

*"I can not at this time Thy purpose see,
but all is well that's done by Thee."*
—Anonymous

It's Monday morning. I awoke at the signal of my alarm clock that sounded like a million cicadas meeting at a chatterbox convention. A severe, earth-pounding headache lulled me to sleep and a riveting pulsating one latched on to my head as I broke forth from the cocoon of my despondency.

I slept, but then again, I didn't. The commercial breaks that reminded me of my impending fate—facing my boss with the bad news—popped up unannounced between my tossing and turning during the night.

Did yesterday happen?

Yes it did!

Was it real?

Most assuredly! It was as real as the pain I tried to suppress during the night. The anguish I experienced knowing I would have to face my colleagues while holding this unbearable secret had overwhelmed me. I just could not imagine myself greeting my boss with such an announcement. I knew I had to let her know first before I would venture to tell those closest to me.

The drive to work seemed a long one. As I turned out of my street, I strained to follow through with my early morning car worship. My hallelujah cheers barely made it to my lips before they were drowned out by quickly forming thoughts of leaving the job under such circumstance.

My "glory praise" squeezed past the unrelenting thoughts of how I was going to face my boss and made it to the doors of my lips just in time. It wasn't the usual loud and robust "Glory," but at least it came out—out far enough to cause a temporary shift in my spirit.

For a minute there, I remembered the promises I made to the Lord to trust Him no matter what the outcome. I even went as far as to begin singing some of my morning car worship songs: "I worship You, Almighty God there is none like you…" "With my hands lifted up, and my mouth filled with praise, with a heart of thanksgiving I will bless Thee, O Lord…" Other songs began to flow easier out of me, now. It was as if I was momentarily transformed into the person I once was before all of this happened.

Slipping in and out of reality seemed to be a common thing to do lately. At one minute I was being ushered into worship; the next minute I was struggling with the fact that I serve God, spend quality time in His presence weekly, teach the adult Bible class at church, lead praise and worship, and now I am being stepped on, dragged through the mud of inferiority and disgrace.

"What have I done to deserve this kind of treatment?" I exclaimed loudly in my mind, but my lips uttered no words. I fought to keep my mind from straying into the areas of unrest and consternation. As I drove down Beltway 495 towards Virginia, I found myself rehearsing the whole story, with plot and characters, as to my fate.

"What will be my boss' reaction?"

"Will others find out and begin the classic rumor mill gossip chain?"

"Will everybody now think I'm dumb?"

"What about my students? Will they find out and then think that I have given up?"

My body began to writhe in pain as I slowly internalized the questions and imagined the answers.

"My God! Do I really have to do this," I said to myself?

"There's got to be another way of getting this formidable responsibility done," I continued.

"Just say it!" Yep, I came to the conclusion to just say it.

The morning conference meeting started with the usual small chatter around the table. I sat there, looking quite pretty; at least that's what a few of my colleagues said prior to sitting down. Feeling and looking pretty meant nothing to me that morning. I was in my old little world. Occasionally, I would scan the room to see if anyone could detect my secret. Not knowing when I would be terminated, I began to look at things as if it were my last day.

As we began to near the end of the meeting, I looked at my boss and said in a soft whisper,

"Do you have some time when we could talk? I really need to share something with you."

Immediately I felt as if she knew exactly what I had to say. It was as if a bolt of energy was zapped from my body. I became weak and nervous as the minutes ticked on to signal the end of the meeting. I began to rustle the papers in front of me and pretended to be busy searching for a student's court report, just to avoid having eye-to-eye contact with anyone.

"Well, what I have for you is bad news..." I said with a tremor rustling beneath my sultry voice.

With very little strength remaining to play the role of the congenial person, I garnered enough energy and said,

"I got my scores back... I missed it by 2 points."

At that announcement, it seemed like a thick black cloud rested over the room and we sat there as if waiting for a thundershower to just break forth. Instead, it was tears and overwhelming words of comfort. She sat there as if stunned by the news of a loved one dying. With elbows on the table and hands at her mouth, she turned pinkish red and the tears began to fall.

"Just 2 points...Only 2 points," she repeated over and over again.

Taking me by the hand and looking me in the eye, she gently said,

"You are one of the best teachers I have ever had the pleasure of working with. I'm going to miss you," she announced.

"What is this place going to be like without you? What about your students? How are they going to handle this?" she asked.

I heard her, but then again, I didn't. As she posed the questions, the tears I had bottled up during the night began to drip one by one from my eyelids to the paper in front of me. I tried catching them before they crashed down with a splash, but my hands weren't fast enough.

I'm scared! I feel bad about having to leave under such a condition—failing a test!" I announced.

"You will leave here with your head up! You have nothing to be ashamed of! You tried your best. Maybe this is God's way to get you ready for full-time ministry" she whispered in a gentle yet firm voice.

What did she just say? "...Full-time ministry?" It went over my head like a 747 jet plane. I heard it, but it meant nothing to me at the time. I tried to smile in agreement, but my face became flushed and my cheeks trembled as the tears flowed unhindered. I tried to muster enough courage to tell my other three friends at work, but I just could not do it. I asked my boss to stay with me as I made my grand announcement.

Did they help the matter any? Not in the least. The tears flowed heavier as they expressed their love and care for me.

"You're an excellent teacher," one said.

Others chimed in with words of admiration and affirmation. After they left the room, Ann said, with lots of love and care in her eyes, but with an assertive tone,

"You're gonna take this test again. We're going to take it until time runs out."

Could I answer her right then and there? Of course not! I was still trying to reel back from exposing my failure to them.

The announcement for breakfast had chimed in on the loud speaker, so we parted quickly without sealing the deal. I worked feverishly to prepare the classroom for the students' arrival, but I felt numb to everything around me. I carried on with my responsibilities, but my mind was in la-la-land.

What a roller coaster ride! I was at peace with my fate and now it seemed I was taking a nosedive right back to the valley of "Why's." It felt like the rug had been pulled from beneath me and I, suspended in mid air, could do nothing to change this new course of action. Help! Help! Help!

What is next in store for me?

"Is there life after a day like this," I wondered as I composed myself to begin the responsibilities of the day.

Six weeks had gone by, and I waited patiently for the outcome of the test, again. In the city of my soul, I felt as though I had done something contrary. I wrestled with, "What if the last time was supposed to be the last time?"

Had I gone against the will of God? Had I ignored His soft promptings, discreet overtures, tender persuasions, and soft push in His direction? I seemed to have been overly concerned about my intellectual status rather than seeking to know His will in the matter.

REFLECTION ON LESSONS LEARNED

←*←*←*←*←*←*←

God processes us through situations, circumstances, and people. Want to move to the next level? Want a change in the mundane things of your life? Well, don't ask God for it unless you are truly ready for a shift, a change…

Learn as much as you can where you are and with what you have available to you. The process can seem like a storm at times, but know that the Captain of "your" ship is in charge.

Here are some lessons I learned from this experience:

- Don't always rush to take failure so personal that you lose sight of the bigger picture.
- Guard/protect your healing, deliverance, and the promises God made to you. I was so pre-occupied with the bad news about my test that I had begun to fall back into a depressed state. I had been delivered and healed of it in the past, but somehow I had begun to relinquish my power over that thing to the devil. Worship helped to bring me back into a healthy mindset. Also, in the interim, God protected my mind.
- If you are uncertain as to what you should do about a thing, spend time seeking God's face for direction. Be still! Wait!
- Know what God is saying to you and stand on it.
- It's okay to make plans, but please leave room for God to make changes as He sees fit.
- Don't ever think that no one is watching your demeanor at work, especially when you profess Christ. Your light of love is what will keep the place safe and secure.

CHAPTER TWELVE

THE SILENT VOICE OF GOD

"There are times when silence has the loudest voice."
—Leroy Brownlow

It was a few days before Christmas 2003. June and I were busy making plans to go to Jamaica, the land of our birth. Tickets were bought, families were contacted, and our luggage were packed. The only thing that was left to do was to pay my hairdresser a visit.

Excitement was settling in, and we contrived ways of getting money out of our siblings for pocket change. None of the things we tried worked, but God blessed us through the giving hearts of Delroy and Patela Oakley. As a matter of fact, they gave me the money, but June helped to spend it.

I had learned enough from all the things that had happened to me up until now. Making the most of the time I have available was truly a great lesson learned. Whenever I could, I shared the gospel with sinner and saint (sometimes it was hard to tell between the two). Okay, I'll leave that one alone.

Anyway, we were in Jamaica for at least a week before we ventured to a vacation spot in Ocho Rios. As we walked to a jerk chicken stand, we ran into this guy who tried to "pick up" June and me. He thought we were one of these "fast" girls. When we began to talk to him about the Lord, his eyes popped open wide, and his mouth hung ajar.

"You' guys are Christians?" he asked.

"You don't look like it to me," he continued.

June and I were dressed appropriately for the weather: beautifully styled hair, sleeveless blouses that rested on the top of our hips, Capri pants, sandals, necklace, bracelets, and yes, suntan lotion.

According to some of the religious standards of the island, we were ladies of the world. When we begun to expound on the Word of God to him, he said,

"Women in my church do not dress that way. Yes, he said "his church." Now here is a "Christian 7th-Day Adventist church going man" hitting on two women of the world, or so he thought.

By the time we were finished with him, he had forgotten which direction he was walking. As a matter of fact, he began making circles before realizing the direction he had been walking initially.

I mention that story because it had such an impact on my mind, I was sure to dream about it. But the opposite happened. I dreamed that I was back in the States at the Fairfax County Juvenile Detention Center. I was standing in a room unfamiliar to me, and I was overhearing a conversation between my Principal, Ann, and her supervisor.

"I'm leaving JDC. I'll be putting in my resignation within the coming week," Ann said.

I couldn't hear clearly what her supervisor was saying to her, but from her response, it sounded as if she was trying to convince her to stay. At that moment, I burst into the room and exclaimed,

"Ann, if you leave, then it's time for me to leave. If you go, then I'm going too!"

Ann held on to my arms and began to beg me not to leave.

"Hewlette, you can't leave here. The kids need you; you're such an inspiration to them and us... You can't leave!"

I jumped up from the dream and sat up in bed pondering what this dream meant. I knew that my principal would not dare resign. I knew she implied, a year before, that she would probably retire from this position. I just knew this dream was too far out there to be real, or was it?

We spent another two weeks in Jamaica and left an indelible impression on the island. I mean we walked the beach. We ate as much Jamaican food we could. We messed with as many crazy fun-loving people we could, and we testified to as many nut cases and obvious sinners as we encountered. Some just listened because they looked at us as "hot chicks" and wanted to take us out on dates. Others listened because we had something legitimate to offer—Jesus. Overall, the trip was memorable, but I just could not shake the dream.

I returned to work to meet my colleagues for the first time in 2004. It appeared that I was sorely missed. I was only gone for two weeks into the New Year and already some were complaining that I had abandoned them. I sat beside Ann for the early morning meeting with my fellow colleagues. After we went through the usual preliminaries and discussed new and incoming students, there was a silence.

This silence didn't really stand out to me until after the event occurred.

"I have an announcement to make," she said in a trembling tone.

"I have officially resigned from being the head of JDC's School Program. I will be here for a few more weeks until someone is hired," she continued.

I didn't hear anything else Ann had to say. Things seemed to move in slow motion for me, and then I heard myself saying,

"I knew this before... I saw this already..."

When I finally shifted from "shock mode" back to the meeting at hand, I realized that it was only Ann and I that were left in the room. I reached out and held her arm, relayed the dream I had in Jamaica, and began shaking my head in disbelief.

"No you can't leave, Hewlette. The kids need you..." she kept saying while holding on to my arms.

Just as I saw in the dream, she replicated it to a tee. I walked to my classroom down the hall as if in a trance. No words could have shaken me out of the phase I was temporarily in.

"My" boys came in; I went through the motions with them... You know, like the pledge of allegiance, a moment of silence, la-di-dah... la-di-dah... But, it was not the same. Everything for me had shifted in the wrong direction; at least that's what it seemed like at the time.

If there was a time when I doubted what my future held, it was after getting the results of the last certification test. Yes, I had decided to take the test again because I felt that this was where I was destined to be. My job was a great place for ministry.

And yes, I knew I was not supposed to engage in religious teachings or deliberations with the students, according to school rules, but whenever the opportunity presented itself for me to teach from a moral perspective with a spiritual undertone, I took advantage of it.

It was only a week after Ann's announcement that I got the results. I "bombed" on the test again. I missed it by two lousy points, *again.*

"I'm not doing this again. No, Sir," I said to myself.

"Forget it. I am through!" I said.

"This test doesn't measure my skill as a teacher. I'm a darn good teacher, and I'm smart, too," I encouraged myself.

I was settled on my decision—No more tests!

After a few weeks rolled by, I decided to break the news to Ann. I told her that this would be my last year at JDC. She began to cry and encourage me to take the test again. I told her that my time was up as the scores had to be in by the end of February to the Fairfax County Board of Education. She said,

"You still have time; you got a couple more weeks."

"That may be true, but it takes 4 to 6 weeks for them to grade your paper and respond with a score. It won't reach them in the time frame given to me," I answered.

We walked away from each other with pensive looks and what seemed to be carefully timed, orchestrated steps. I was settled in my decision. Nothing could change the path that had been determined for me; at least not right now.

The phone in my classroom rang. It was Ann asking me to come to her office. As I entered she said,

"Okay, Hewlette, you have until June to successfully pass the test. Remember, you only need a few points."

I guess she noticed the look of consternation on my face because she said,

"You're going to take the test again!"

I stood there in disbelief. First, I had already come to some closure about what my future would be as it related to working for Fairfax County Public Schools. Secondly, I had already begun putting my thoughts together for my resignation letter. And thirdly, I was satisfied that I had told all the right people and didn't need to express anything else to anyone.

Ann, with her precious ways and unusual contacts, had made calls and provided me the opportunity to take the test before June 2004. I looked at Ann while she gathered the paperwork for me to register for the test and said,

"Are you sure you're not forcing the hand of God on this?"

"Look, Hewlette, I know you're called to go into ministry, but for right now you need money and health insurance. At least work another year, save up the money, and then resign," she said firmly.

Sounded great, but I was still uncomfortable with it. I gave in, though, and resumed studying for the tests again. Pat and Amy (dear colleagues and friends of mine) found out and quickly volunteered to pay for the examinations.

The act of studying was never a problem for me; it was that I had to study Math. I had done great on the English tests, but it was not enough to cover the points I was missing on the math portion. Furthermore, I'm an English teacher, not a Math genius! Well, this time, I was determined to beat this thing with a vengeance, especially in light of the fact that they all believed I could do it. But then again, it was Math!

All my life I ran away from Math because my brain could not comprehend it as a youngster. The highest grade I ever received in a Math class was a "B," and that was an Introduction to Algebra class. I had a great teacher, Mr. Wright, in 12th grade. All my other Math teachers just skipped right over me as if I didn't matter. I used to answer the questions wrong and do poorly on quizzes and tests, but none of them stopped to figure out why. The first and only "F" I ever received was in Math—High School Geometry.

In college, as part of my Political Science curriculum, I had to take Statistics. Now that was a killer, but I had a wonderful teacher, Dr. Bakshi. I was four of thirty students to get a "C" in his class. There were two "A's", six "B's," and the rest were downhill from there. That "C" was like an "A" to me. Math was such a dreaded thing that I would tell people, "Every time I see numbers, my brain locks."

The students I taught would sometimes ask me why I tried so hard with them, even when they didn't care themselves. I would pull up a chair, sit down right in front of them, and tell them my story about Math and the "mean, uncaring, busy" teachers I had. Furthermore, I didn't want them to have the same perception of me as I had of my Math teachers.

Well, what does all of this have to do with "The Silent Voice of God?" Well, everything! God was talking to me, but was I listening? He was talking to me about my future, the test, and the next move... But was I truly listening? Was I patched into the same frequency on which He was broadcasting? Let's read on and see.

CHAPTER THIRTEEN

CONTEMPLATION

"God moves in mysterious ways, but He's always moving."
—Anonymous

It was on a cold winter's morning in February 2004 that I felt something unusual stirring in my heart. It was as if my mind was very busy during the night as I slept and now my heart was conversing with my mind to catch up on the night's events. What was it that captured the very nerves of my being? Was something coming down the road that would affect the comfortable life style I had built up for myself?

Well, I did not know it at the time, but God was moving out some of the <u>furniture</u> of my life—lack of total reliance, using the past to judge the present, second guessing God, the need to know now—in order to create a void only He could fill. To start the day of just right, I quickly shifted gears and began to sort out my day to suit my fancy.

I was nearing the end of the quarter in which I taught poetry, and I had assigned a word from which every one was to write at least a two-stanza poem using that word. One of my students, after some deliberation with the rest of the class, convinced the majority that the word "contemplation" would be a great word on which to write.

"Okay class, go ahead and just write freely without thinking of syntax, mechanics…" I said in order to challenge their thinking.

"As a matter of fact, I'm not a poet, but I'm gonna join you. I'll do the same thing that I'm asking you to do," I informed them.

After about eight minutes of writing, erasing, scratching, and panicking, we began sharing our poems. I must say the students did very well. I was a bit timid about sharing mine after hearing what they wrote, but they coaxed me into doing it.

"Okay, listen up you William Shakespeares, Robert Frosts, Walt Whitmans, Langston Hughes, and so on," I announced.

"Don't judge me 'cause I'm your teacher. Right now I'm just like you," I begged.

"Come on, Ms. Pearson, let's have it," they said.

"I bet yours is better than ours… Come on, let's hear it," some shouted.

Now you must realize that these kids are not the typical public school students. No sir. I teach in a juvenile detention facility, specifically junior high to high school boys. It was likely that I would not see these students again. I surely did not want them to remember me by a poorly written poem. Surely not!

"We're waiting, Ms. Pearson," interrupted the silent conversation I had going on in my head.

With a tad bit of trepidation I said,

"Okay, boys, here it goes…"

Contemplation

Like an oracle without a command
I sit and ponder the road ahead.
Breaking through the silence I hear a pop
It was my heart beating as if a clock.

> *Pensive, I see the images so clear*
> *A forked road and a hand pointing there.*
> *"Take this one or that one," what a choice*
> *I think I'll heed to my inner voice.*

There was perfect silence as I approached the last word in the poem. I slowly lifted my head from the reading position and positioned my eyes to the top edge of the paper. Silence! Not a motion or response was heard. I looked at each of my students (12 in all) and waited for them to laugh, but all I could see was confusion on their faces.

"Aaah, come on, you guys. Don't tell me it's not great," I said.

"That ain't it, Ms. Pearson. We don't get it. It's too deep for us," they all chimed in. In my defense I said,

"Well, at least I wrote a poem and I think it's a good one."

Doesn't God just move *"... in mysterious ways, His wonders to perform?"* The fact that God was moving was enough for me. But to know that He would use a teaching strategy to wake me up was just mind-boggling.

Go ahead and read the poem again. This time, think about the fact that I had been struggling to figure out what was going on inside of me. Trying to find answers to address that unnerving feeling I had earlier that morning.

What about the last stanza? It surely speaks of the fact that God was talking to me. I know He was speaking and encouraging me to heed the inner voice—His inner voice.

Well maybe I haven't told you yet, but I had been seeking the Lord, asking Him to tell me exactly what to do regarding my future, my livelihood, my income, the great plans He had for my life. I had already thought of leaving the job, but knew I needed to get God's okay first.

In the fall of the previous year, I had sought the Lord regarding taking the certification tests or leaving to do something else. I knew that that "something else" was ministry, but I just did not want to face it. Here I was, an intelligent young lady who had great plans for her life. I endured much—many difficult work assignments— in graduate school, so I could be the best teacher possible. Give that up? No way!

Then on one occasion I heard the voice of God say, "I know you are waiting for answers... and they will come... I will speak to you, but it will not be in the manner you are used to. It may appear that I am silent, but I am not."

Excited, confident, enthused, hopeful, and content I was? Not in the least. I wanted to know things now! I needed to know what was around the corner and down the road. I liked to plan for things and at this juncture in my life an eye into the future was definitely necessary; at least that's what I thought.

The poem... Was this the "different" manner God alluded to in His remarks to me? I toyed with the idea as I wrestled with whether or not to take the tests again if the outcome was not favorable. I also contemplated resigning from the job. My colleagues did not make it easy for me. They were willing to do whatever it took to get me to pass that math test. What a tough decision, or was it?

I had called home one afternoon just to check on my Mom. Dad answered the phone and for some strange reason, he and I started talking about the test.

"Hewlette, I was thinking about it the other day and said, 'What if Hewlette's time is up at that place? Maybe this is her season to leave,' " he said.

Well, needless to say I was awestruck. My Dad doesn't usually say much when it comes to involving himself in the decision making process of his grown children. Therefore, when he said that, it really took me for a loop. I even stopped for a minute and said,

"God, are you talking to me through my Dad?"

Several weeks later, I got the results, but not before I jumped ahead and took the tests all over again—just in case this one did not work out for me. This time, the scores were worst than ever. I did poorly on the English test and missed the Math section by two points.

Talking about a slap in the face! The very subject I taught in school... The one thing I knew I was quite good in... The very thing that proved to me that I was a scholar in mine own right now shattered every positive image I had of myself.

"God! What are You doing to me!!!" I screamed.

"You could have told me. You could have spared me from this! You could have protected my reputation!"

"Why?"

Somehow, I started having flashbacks on conversations I had with friends and family. A good friend of mine, Patela, called one morning as I was on my way to take the test. She wished me well, but then said,

"Hewlette, I think God is trying to tell you this is it. Maybe He's calling you to do something else..."

I heard her, but my actions proved I truly did not. Even my sister, Julianne, talked to me at length one morning on my way to work about doing what God had called me to do.

"Girl, I don't know, but maybe God wants you to share His word with a different crowd... Maybe He's calling you to ministry..." she encouraged.

"Yes, I know, you're probably right," I responded. But the conviction about "this thing" was not there.

Spring Break was fast approaching, but not fast enough. I needed some answers. I needed a break away from everything and everyone that reminded me of school and those tests. I decided this would be a good time to seek the Lord—again— as to what I should do.

My colleagues were encouraging me to hold out for the next scores,

"If they are not good, you'll take it again until the scores get better," they said.

I thought about it. Yes, I truly thought long and hard about it. In resignation I said,

"You know what? I feel that this is not what God wants me to do."

Did I sound convicted? Not really. I know I was not because I kept flip-flopping on the idea.

I went to Philadelphia, Pennsylvania to get away from it all. As I was about to wake up from my night's rest, I was ushered back into the dream I had when I vacationed in Jamaica. I jumped up from the covers and announced, "Lord, that dream wasn't about Ann, it's about me... It's for me..."

I sat up in the bed and began to question God.

"Why didn't You let me know You were talking to me?"

"Why weren't You clearer with your directions?"

Well by now, I know you think I'm crazy to be talking to God like that, but my relationship with Him set the tone for me to be honest with Him and myself. I was thinking it anyway, so I thought it not disrespectful to say it aloud.

"You were listening with your ears and not your heart," a gentle and caring voice said.

It came from deep within my spirit. It seemed it had been stirring for a while... It was like the opportunity was waiting in the wings all along, just to exhale those embracing words. God was talking to me all along, but I was listening with my ears—my physical ears that is. I was eagerly waiting for a resounding, earth moving, confident cheering,

"Thou shalt do this..."

"Thou shalt not go this way..."

"Thou wilt get this for doing this..."

God's soft promptings in my heart were easily ignored. I relegated His moving to a small box, the size of my mind. Only what I could hear, audibly, see obviously, and feel nearby were of interest to me.

I was not stretching the mind of my spirit to know that the dreams I was having were Him speaking to me. The unsettled feelings and unusual stirrings I felt in my heart were God talking to me in a "different" way. My family and friends who encouraged me to consider another path were physical guideposts God provided to me. And I did not realize that some of the very words that came out of my mouth were prophetic towards to myself.

The answers were there all along. I was speaking them to myself, in a haphazard kind of way, and did not see the importance or the unique relevance at the time. The Holy Spirit was very active in all of this, but I was yielding to the familiarities of the flesh.

"Lord, I thank You for your patience towards me!"

I say it now. I say it always. Imagine. I could have saved all that money I wasted on the tests. I could have used the time I studied to do something profitable for Him. And I could have avoided the embarrassment I inflicted on my own self when I totally bombed on the English portion of the test.

"Lord, I thank You for Your patience towards me!"

I could list a page and a half of other things I could have accomplished. I could have saved myself from a lot of emotional stress if I were more in tuned to the voice of God. Mind you, God was always speaking, but my "antenna" was not tuned to pick up His frequency. My receptors were pointing in the direction of my own self-will and confidence. I listened for the "radio waves" of the Holy Spirit, but did not trust the signal because it was not familiar.

I know that I am not the only one that has ever missed the signs of God's purpose. Yes, we hear the rustling, the shifting, and sometimes feel the nudging, but for some reason we seem to run right pass the indicators that point to the right direction.

Yes, we may have heard a voice and wondered who was talking. We may have even heard a whisper, but continued on our way. Guess what? We are not alone. First Samuel 3:1-10 gives a wonderful picture of a little lad who heard a voice calling, calling in the night. He thought it was the voice of the priest. He ran to Eli, the priest, each time and said, "Here am I."

He did this for three times before the priest realized that it was the Lord that was calling little Samuel. Although Eli was getting old and could no longer see well, he had the presence of mind to give Samuel the best instruction ever: *"When you hear the voice calling again, say,' Speak, Lord; for thy servant heareth.'"*

That short sentence speaks volumes to anyone who is waiting on the Lord for something, for an answer. "Speak, Lord" uncovers for me the lies and deceit the enemy thought would crush the will of the Father in my life. It assures the waiting soul that only the voice of God can make a difference. It bellows a confidence that only His will can prevail! And it signals that the hearer has submitted his wants and desires to the Lordship of Christ. Basically it's saying,

"Whatever You desire, Father, that I will do…"

"Whatever seems right to You, I will embrace…"

"I am transparent before You now…and I'm listening…"

"I am trusting You this time… and I'm following…"

"Your voice makes the difference!"

"Your voice makes the difference!"

"Your voice makes the difference!"

Now you may wonder what was the big deal about Samuel hearing the voice of God at such an early age. Well, it was a huge deal, as the scripture tells us, *"And the word of the Lord was precious in those days; there was no open vision"* (1 Samuel 3:1). To put it bluntly—God was not speaking or showing himself to anyone in Israel. Israel's communication line to Heaven had been disconnected for a very long time.

Imagine existing without knowing which road to take. Think about how it must have been to want to get direction regarding a matter and no help was around. Go into the corridors of your mind and try to imagine yourself praying, fasting, and meditating, but the God you served was not visibly listening, responding, or giving approval to your acts of worship.

What an empty life that must have been! What a loss of divine blessing! What promises went unfulfilled! What a futile future they must have faced without God's providence!

So you see it was refreshing to hear God speaking again. It did not matter if it were a blessing or disappointing news. What mattered most was that God spoke. His speaking meant that there was still hope. There was still a chance that the gracious promises He covenanted with Abraham would yet come to pass. The hearing of God's voice decreed that He had been there all along watching, orchestrating, maneuvering, and ensuring that His will would prevail.

You've got to read the rest of the story just to see how mightily God used Samuel to bring the people's heart back to God. But back to me…

Finally, I now understood that the dream was for me, not my boss. The voice of God echoed through the channel of a dream. It was His voice leading me into un-chartered territories. He was choreographing my steps to the beat of His song.

Now to break the news to my colleagues! "What am I going to say," I thought. It was not an easy task that lay in front of me, but I knew that they, like me, were waiting for an answer. My answer came. It came at a time when it was so precious to me. It was not what they were looking for, but after talking with them, they agreed that they would respect my decision and support me; at least that is what they said in my presence.

Knowing the love and care they have for me, I'm more inclined to think that they gathered together and discussed the matter in little groups. Some probably said,

"I love Hewlette and all, but I think she is waaaay off base with this one…"

"Well, I figured she would end up doing something like this, but I don't know if the timing is right…"

"How's she going to manage? What about health insurance? She's got an interesting health track record… I'm scared for her…"

"You know what? Hewlette is going to be fine… I think?"

"Let's leave it alone, she'll probably change her mind."

Such great folks to work with! I mean that with all the love I have for them.

Writing my letter of resignation and actually mailing it was not easy. Of course I had already made up my mind to leave, but the actual act was not as easy as the decision. On the "Separation Form" there were categories to choose from as to why one was leaving the school system: resignation in lieu of termination; retirement, termination; resignation; one year leave of absence; other.

The reality of what I was about to do hit me like a cement truck driven by a five year old. I struggled with what category to choose. Of course "other" was looking mighty good to me, but I just could not keep my eyes off "resignation in lieu of termination." Wasn't it exactly what I was doing? Would I be considered a coward for not taking the test to the very end?

Well, "resignation" was the winner. I checked the box and wrote this explanation on the line provided—"resigning to go into full time ministry." What? Where under God's blue heavens did that come from?

Part-time ministry has been a part of my life for some time now. Traveling up and down the Northeast corridor of Interstate I-95, preaching, conducting seminars, praise and worship workshops, and services had its toll on me at times. I enjoy ministering to God's people, but the exhaustion that follows can be overwhelming, especially with a full time job.

Me in full time ministry? Yeah, right! This part-time ministry stuff, at times, had taken a bite out of my purse, so I knew doing it full-time would just swallow me and my entire pocketbook. It probably would occasionally burp up a buck or two, but that would be it. Depending on others to support me was not the road I had imagined in my future. Therefore, doing full-time ministry was totally out of the question.

I filled out the necessary paperwork and mailed them off. Such sweet relief swept over me that I felt like I had gained momentum for the next "test." I felt like I had won a million pennies, ooops, I mean dollars. This thing had truly weighed me down, and I realized that the plans I made each year were centered on making time to study for the certification tests.

The way is clear; the door of opportunity is wide open for God to do whatever He pleases with my life. Yes, my scores are currently good enough for me to teach in other jurisdictions, i.e., Maryland, Washington, D.C., etc. But that is not what God is leading me to do. Everything is not clear yet, but my future looks brighter than it has ever been.

Oh by the way, the test scores from the last tests I took came back. Guess what? I... Does it matter?

REFLECTION ON LESSONS LEARNED

←*←*←*←*←*←*←

This chapter revealed a lot of what was going on in my mind. I wrestled with what God planned for my life and what I had envisioned for my own future. But, I realized that the plan of God for my life had been predestined before I was ever born. Everything I did up to this point prepared me for this awesome leap of faith. Every individual who invested time by being friends with me poured something positive into my life to help me get to this point.

I am learning that resting in my trust of Him is where my success lies. It is a wonderful decision I have come to, for it solidifies, stabilizes, and reinforces all the thoughts and feelings that were dancing in the marshes of my doubts.

One of the great many lessons that I learned from this experience is that I was already certified and approved.

- God had already qualified me by placing me in one of the best school systems in the nation.
- He had allowed me to work there for five years without "man's" certification approval.

This is a great testimony to the mighty hand of God. According to the laws of the Virginia Board of Education, a new teacher is required to have his or her certification documents completed before the end of their third year. However, the Board continued to renew my contract each year without question. Favor! Favor! Favor!

I realize more now than ever that I was placed at that school specifically by God to be a source of comfort, light, healing, encouragement, wisdom, cheer, and laughter. Not only so, I was also there to be poured into by some beautiful colleagues who taught me to respect and embrace the gift God gave me and to pursue the path He ordained for my life.

The challenges that I faced with the students and some of the faculty members pressed me against the mirror of heaven so I could see the "real" Hewlette. Guess what? The image was wonderful. I met every challenge with fortitude and remained faithful to my profession and my Christian integrity.

Learning the voice of the Lord in this particular season was pivotal to my making the right decision:

- The fact that I trust the direction He is taking me proves that I have begun to hear Him with my heart instead of only with my ears.

- Not surrendering fully prolongs the process and can take us off the path of our success.
- Allowing the past to dictate our future can have a devastating effect on our faith.
- God uses people and things to teach, show, and prove His desires for our lives.

We must truly understand that God is a God of creativity and beauty. He shows us through the lovely flora and fauna of the earth. But all that beauty would not be possible without the earth going through its seasons. Like the earth, our life has seasons.

I learned that my season at this job was over. It was now time for me to grow from the experiences I encountered there. The seeds of maturity, love, selflessness, patience, kindness, and longsuffering that had been planted needed a place to shoot out their lovely buds. They needed a place to spread their leaves and vines and to give off a sweet and refreshing aroma.

So never despair when you feel the wind of change is blowing. Secure the hatch of your faith, lean and hold on to the helm of time, and steady your feet in the promises of God. The waves of life's disappointment will dash, and the billows of impatience will leave a mist of doubt. But be encouraged. You will not be misguided. God will see to it that you are secure and safe.

Trust Him and enjoy the voyage!

CHAPTER FOURTEEN

A LEAP OF FAITH:
I'M SCARED BUT...

"Be not afraid of tomorrow, the Lord is already there..."
—Anonymous

I remember the stories of the many patriarchs we studied in our "little children's" Bible class on early Saturday mornings in church. We learned about father Abraham, Moses, David and Goliath, Gideon, Joseph, Ruth, Samson, Daniel and the three Hebrew boys, Samuel, Jeremiah, Esther, Caleb and Joshua, Job, and others. Interestingly though, the majority of them were men. They all lived victorious lives and showed great faith towards God, but what about the women of the Bible?

Growing up, I needed someone of the female gender to relate to. So as I and my brothers became scholars of the Old Testament (we just loved reading all those strange stories) at a very young age, I found myself scouring the Old Testament for women who were wise, strong in character, and who could stand up right along side any of those great male patriarchs. Forget about those women who were weak, devious, manipulative, and stubborn (although there is much you can learn from them). But I was on a terrific journey to find a precious woman, a woman of character, spiritual muscles, and full of favor.

Well, I found some: Deborah, Abigail, Huldah, the widow of Zarephath, Manoah's wife, Hannah, Rahab, the Shunammite woman, Hagar, Leah, and others. I learned so many wonderful lessons from these women that if they were alive today, they would probably say to me, "You go girl!" Some of the names maybe unfamiliar to you so get out your Bible and read about them. They have some very interesting stories to tell that will capture your attention. And soon you'll agree with me.

One woman in particular that was not mentioned is Sarah, the wife of Abraham. I purposely did not include her in the list because her life is not chronicled in detail as some of the women mentioned. But I gained great insight from what is not stated. If you will allow me to use my imagination, I will let my thoughts become transparent to you. The scene probably went like this....

Abraham hears a powerful yet gentle and compelling voice say,

"Abram, Abram!" (Their names were Abram and Sarai at the time.)

Abram, busy tending the flock of sheep, is suddenly startled. Turning in every direction to see who called him and seeing no one, he returns to shearing the wool of a sheep. With each stroke of his hand against the sparsely matted coat of the sheep, he occasionally looks to the left and then to the right as if expecting someone.

"Abram!"

As if given a sudden burst of energy, Abram jumps up, knocks over the stool, spills the basin of water, bends over, and wrestles to stabilize the shearing table as the tools go flying. He stands still in fear for a moment, and then, as if in slow motion, raises his torso to an upright position while clutching the sheep's wool to his chest.

"Y-e-s," he answered with a quiver in his voice.

Abram looks in the direction of the voice as he tries to balance his left leg against the tent peg in order to appear stoic. With eyes squinted, he lifts the wool to his brow to block the brightness of the noonday sun. He listens intently.

"Get up. Leave your family. Leave this land. Go to another land. This land you will go to is unfamiliar to you. You do not know where it is or what it looks like. But you will be blessed," the voice said.

Can you imagine the look on Abram's face when he heard that? Forget about the look. How about the thoughts that probably rushed through his mind? I'm sure he probably thought about how he would have to leave his father, mother, brothers, nieces, nephews, cousins, and friends.

How about missing out on some of the camp's favorite past times: staff wrestling, sheep shearing contests, cattle-carrying marathons... But more importantly, how was he going to explain leaving and not being able to tell them where he was going.

Here is Abram. He is told to leave a land he knows so well to go to somewhere he has never been before. What utter madness is this? What strange and immeasurable request was this? I will venture to say that for some of us, this would be totally out of the question.

"No way 'Jose' would I get up and go to some place I've never heard of or been to before... What! I move on the recommendation of some great voice out of heaven that had no body attached to it?" some of us would mumble in our minds.

"Yes, He said He would show me, but what if He doesn't even know the way?" others would think.

God acknowledged that Abram knew the land where he was living very well. But God understood what emotional and psychological toll this would have on his mind and body. God also chose Abram based upon His knowledge of Abrams potential to follow Him wholly.

But the great revelation I received from reading the beginning part of God's dialogue with Abram is this: When God acknowledged that Abram knew the land well, He knew and saw the great risk Abram would have to take—so He tells him about the blessings.

God knows our human needs and desires. Our wanting to succeed at life's tasks… Our desire to be prosperous in everything we do… The dreams and aspirations we have that fuel our endeavors. Yes! God shifted Abram's mind to the blessings.

Blessings. Blessings. Blessings. Just hearing the word alone sends a shiver of hope in a believer's ear. So often we get excited about the blessings of Jesus Christ that we sometime forget about all the cares and troubles that were stacked up against us. We begin to jump and shout for joy knowing that a great promise has begun to shift us from the place of fantasy to the realms of reality.

Abram probably became excited there for a minute, too, but that was soon quenched by thoughts of, "How am I going to tell Sarai about this?" I can see the wheels of Abram's mind turning… turning… turning… And an eyebrow lifting… Falling… Falling at the likely possibilities of rejection and nonacceptance.

He got up, brushed off the residue of wool from his tunic, caught fresh water and washed his face in the basin, combed his hair, lifted his staff, and set off to have a talk with Sarai. The entire trip lasted only a few minutes, but it seemed like hours for Abram as he ran through every possible scenario with each heavy step towards the entrance of the kitchen tent.

Being a female, I know that women tend to be a little more supportive, understanding, and caring than men. Men, don't stone me, but it's true, admit it! But you've got to be kidding me if you say that you believe Sarai was cool with this when Abram first came to her with the idea... Ooops, I mean decision. Allow me to paint a picture of what possibly took place when Abram arrived home.

"Honey, Sugar Plum, Sweetie Pie, Luscious Cheeks... I got something to tell you. Hon, I have to leave everything and everybody, except for you, Sweetie, and go to another land," he said in one breath in hopes that she probably did not hear every single word.

I can see Sarai dropping the kneading bowl and holding on to the wheat flour paste as if she was squeezing the life out of Abraham.

"You mean we have to get up and move again? We just got here, Abram," she exclaimed.

"Your father rooted us up out of our last home in Ur; we're barely settled and you say, 'let's go.' Does your Dad know about this," she asked?

Before Abraham could get a word in edgewise, Sarai quickly chimed,

"Your father said we'll eventually move to Canaan, but for right now living here in Haran suits him just fine. How are you going to explain this one to him?"

I can see the sweat beading up on Sarai's forehead and Abram nervously holding on to his staff for dear life while anticipating her next question—

"Well, where are we moving to this time?"

A silent hush rushed into the tent where they stood together. Abram could no longer hear the crying of the sheep in the background; he could no longer rely on the crowing of the hens or the crackling of the wood in the fire to take the attention off his nervousness.

He looked around to see if there were anyone else nearby and then whispered,

"I don't know, Sweetie, but Sarai, I need you to trust me on this one."

"Abram Honey, are you sure?" Sarai said with the warmth and care of a loving wife.

With a twinkle in his eye and a bright smile on his face, he painstakingly, yet assuredly said,

"Sweetheart, Sarai, Woman of my dreams... God said He'll make me the father of a great nation; He will bless me, make me famous, and make me a blessing to other people."

"Honey, that's not all," he exclaimed.

"God also said that anybody who blessed me would be blessed and anyone who cursed me would be cursed. He said the whole world would be blessed because of me," Abram said in a reassuring, yet exuberant voice.

They embraced each other as if in agreement, then suddenly, a wild baby goat pushed his way in between them and interrupted the conversation between their hearts. Abram, with a level of confidence that came from the support of his wife and being refreshed by the beauty of her presence, walked towards the door of the tent, stopped, turned, and winked at Sarai. His steps were lighter now; he no longer hesitated to tell his family the news.

As soon as his shadow vanished from the entrance of the tent, Sarai drops to the floor and pulls her legs up so that her head could rest on her knees. She begins to rock back and forth while singing one of those Chaldean songs the maidens used to sing when gathered at the well. "I don't know how we're gonna do it, but it's got to be done... We might not be able to see the light of day, but we'll just keep drawing... pulling...moving on..."

Now I know the Bible did not go into the details like I just did, but I can assume it possibly happened that way because they were human and had feelings, emotions, issues, setbacks, reservations, and confusion at times—just as you and me. Understanding this, we can really relate to the fact that they took risks, struggled with family's opinion, and depended on each other for support and strength.

Sarai trusted the voice that spoke to Abram and she trusted her husband's decision. Even if she had any reservations in her heart, she showed him the utmost love and respect to follow him blindly. If she thought it a mistake, it was one she was willing to make with him. If she thought the journey might lead to nowhere, she was willing to be nowhere with Abram.

Now that's a sister with faith, character, fortitude, muscles, and influence!

It's amazing. The great God of heaven took note of Sarai's faith, her willingness to follow her husband, and her commitment to him. As a token of their faithfulness and as a sign of the covenant God made with Abram, both their names were changed: Abram became *Abraham* and Sarai became *Sarah*.

For Sarai, it was no more about the "I" in her name, her personality and character. It was now about the "H" that was added for humility, honor, and holiness. Her promise was attached to her faith all along. They (promise and faith) being companions in arms, worked together to affect her purpose and her destiny.

Now how does that story relate to my situation? Well, I told you before that these great women's actions taught me some great and invaluable lessons. Here's one—when I do not yield to the plan of God on my life, I will forever be living from a mental suitcase, always wondering what's next, always in transition, living an unfulfilled life, running away from my purpose.

God has shown me, through their examples, that I cannot be who He has called me to be if I am comfortable living in a place that I should not be—a place I know so well. When I say place, I do not mean only a physical location. It should be understood that this applies to my mental and spiritual condition. When I refuse to move, the familiar sets in and I find myself <u>not</u> doing what I should be doing.

It is normal for me to want to stay in the familiar, to hold on to what I know best. It is comforting to be prepared knowing what is coming up ahead. Such normal behavior solidifies the foundation of "I'm in control," and therefore, the stage of "rest" is set to display an awesome death—complacency.

Yes, it is normal to want to be the "man," the woman who has it all together. I say "normal" here because that is how many of us operate. If it's done often enough, it becomes routine, normal. But when I begin to do those things that go against the natural flow of my routine, I step into the *abnormal*. It is unusual when I begin to step out on faith and believe what God says I have, I am, and shall be even when nothing remotely resembles it. It's abnormal to give up the controls of our lives to God.

The mercy seat of God is not overcrowded with people waiting to do something because God says so. There are not many who will trust Him blindly and completely. Neither is there many who will stand still long enough to hear and see what He is saying.

When we listen, believe, and do what God says, even when it goes against our better judgment, that's abnormal. That's insane. And that's wonderful.

TAKING THE LEAP

We are often faced with great opportunities that are the stepping-stones that help to bring the dreams and aspirations we have envisioned come to pass. But without expectation, we will never recognize the opportunities as stepping-stones. We will simply construe them as ethereal—something that is absurd, ridiculous, unheard of, or crazy. We, therefore, miss out on a mighty move of God to bring Him glory and us much joy.

When we begin to focus all our efforts on the goal, bring all our thoughts under the control of what our spirit has been yearning and thirsting for, and allow our entire being to be filled up with possibilities that seem to elude the limits of time, then and only then will an atmosphere of opportunity be created. In essence, the heavenly formula for success is this: **expectancy plus opportunity equals the fulfillment of the promise.**

This formula helps to set the stage for something wonderful to take place. The very fiber of our being begins to line up with what was originally ordained from the beginning. Then, the essential parts that make up the "faith" of expectation begin to sing and dance about like a group of 5-year-olds on Christmas Eve. We sense a phenomenal end is near.

But guess what? It sometimes takes its time in coming. It's as if someone directed it to stand backstage and wait for the signal. But in all the waiting, we still can see it. We can smell it. We can taste the brush of victory as it occasionally peeps through the curtains of our imagination.

Come to pass? It will not! Not before time. The stage must be set for it to materialize. The season of its release must be present for it to come forth in a matured form. For when it comes, it must be embraced and accepted by our will, our desire, and our faith.

As we wait, sometimes we find ourselves forgetting the awesome promises, the faithful sayings of our Lord, and the dreams that motivated us. So what does God do? He gives us snapshots of what He is able to do through us when we follow His soft promptings. He gives us little commercial breaks that help to give us the confidence and fortitude needed to take the first, second, or third step.

I remember the morning the Lord said, "Double for your trouble." It is as clear to me today as when it was spoken eight years ago. I have been waiting, waiting, waiting and waiting. But as you have learned, my waiting has not been one of drudgery, boredom, and sole discouragement. On the contrary, many things have occurred to push me back, to light up my day, to have me come out wielding an axe, *and* to push me to the next level.

Each experience also taught me invaluable lessons. Yes, I have experienced trouble, but I believe with all my heart that my "double" is restless nearby, like a racehorse in the starting gate. The atmosphere is set. The air is thick with an aroma of victory. And my "double" is set to break forth, but not yet. Hold your horses!

When we decide to take the risk—move out on a limb and a prayer—and disregard what others might say or think, then we stand on the proper grounds to ask and believe God for the abnormal and "strange" things we desire. For me, they are things that I initially thought were unattainable, but those same things now seem possible, accessible, and real.

Sounds good? Yes it does, but it requires a great deal of self-denial. My friends are watching, my colleagues are concerned about me, and some of my family is wishing for the best with one eye closed and the other open for a "just in case."

I am ready to move out like Sarah and Abraham. I am ready to prove God's word. I hang on His every promise. Will He be there at the finish line? Will He be in the stands cheering me on?

A beautiful friend of mine had this Zen Buddhist quote affixed to her refrigerator, which read, "Leap and the net will appear." That's powerful! That's faith! That's me!

You've gotten the translation already, and I know you're about to shout and cheer for me. But before you do, let me share an encouraging anecdote with you. It's true and so appropriate for this stage of my journey up the mountain.

I have come to the conclusion that children are mouth-pieces for God. They will just tell it to you without hesitation, reservation, or thought for your feelings. They'll come by unannounced, screech right on up into your conversation, and "stick it to you" like it is! That's right, that's children for you—the mouthpiece of God.

Well, I've had many experiences with God talking to me through some of these little people. Yes, I said little people 'cause they and God got some kind of two-way conversation going on that grown folks just can't seem to be able to tap into. I tell you it's amazing.

You know what's funny though? When they get older, it seems they forget about that relationship and power and then have to ask God, "Lord, reveal yourself to me. Let me hear your voice. Help me to see you clearly..." Yes indeed, I know that's true 'cause it's the prayer I've been praying all my life. Amen? Amen!

Back to my story... My 9-year-old nephew at the time, Al 2 (his real name is Aldean II) was busy playing video games with his twin sister, Alayna, down in the den of their home one summer afternoon. I had only stopped by for a brief visit, but ended up spending the entire week with them. Now that I look back, I realized that God had orchestrated that to teach me some valuable lessons... Of course this is one of them I'm about to tell you.

Well on this particular day, both he and his sister were busy competing against each other. Alayna had already eaten, and I noticed that Al 2 had not come upstairs for his lunch yet. I called out to him,

"Hey Al 2, do you want some buffalo wings?"

He shouted, "Oh yeah, Auntie Hewie."

His Mom, Julianne, and I were in the kitchen talking and she had begun to prepare macaroni and cheese. Yes, that all too famous gold and blue box mixture that just sends shivers of delight to every adolescent taste bud. Yum! Yum!

I put some wings on Al 2's plate with potato rolls and somewhat hid the plate from view to trick him. While chomping on a few wings myself, I called out to him,

"Hey Al, it's ready!"

Suddenly there was a rustle, a pattering of two size 13 feet coming up the stairs. As his feet hit the last platform of the steps, I met him half way between the hall and the entrance to the kitchen and said,

"Oops, Al 2, I ate the wings you wanted!"

He jumped passed me into the kitchen, looked at his Mom, turned back, and exclaimed,

"That's okay, Auntie Hewie, Mom's fixing macaroni and cheese."

"You don't care about the wings, Al 2," I responded with a disappointed voice.

"No, Auntie Hewie, that's what I love right there, yum, yum," he proclaimed over and over again while moving his body in rhythmic gyrations.

It was if he was saying,

"You thought you had me, but my Momma got you instead!"

With honey mustard buffalo chicken wing sauce drooling down the sides of my mouth and with chicken bones in hand, I began jumping up and down in the kitchen. I said to Al 2 and Julianne,

"Don't you see it? It's just like the devil to offer us something he thinks we will settle for, but God knows what we love and desire most."

Julianne stood there stirring the contents in the pot, shaking her head and saying,

"My Lord! My Lord!"

I looked at Al 2 and noticed he had not a clue about what just took place, so I restated the analogy to him.

"Okay, Al, when the devil offers you something that looks great, God's got what for you?" I asked.

He quickly shouted,

"Macaroni and cheese!"

Well, that was it for me. I fell out laughing and praising God. What am I trying to say here? Well to me, I saw God saying,

"Look Auntie Hewie, what I got for you is better than what the devil tries to pretty up to offer or try to convince you is better. I know exactly what you like and what you desire most, 'cause I placed those desires in you. Come on now, just trust me...I got your back on this!"

Well, maybe God doesn't speak in that kind of vernacular, but by the time I decoded it for my understanding, He was speaking loud and clear.

I got the picture! I smell the rain coming! The rain of my destiny... The rain of my expected end... The rain of His glory... The rain of my anointing... The rain of His blessings... The rain of the evidence of my faith...

I can hear you cheering now. I can see you waving those banners as the great Band Master signals you to shout and cheer,

"I will not be swayed..."

"I will not be denied my blessing, my destiny..."

"And I will not be distracted from the course planned just for me."

And so like my sister, Sarah of the Old Testament, I jump! I fly! I leap into the will of God!

See you on the other side of my faith!

CHAPTER FIFTEEN

ENCOUNTERING GOD IN VULNERABILITY

"If I show you my weakness,
will you be strengthened or crushed?"
—H.A. Pearson

A re you there yet? I mean on the other side of my faith. I'm here just bursting to tell you about what God has done since I took that leap of faith. It has been two years now since I wrote the chapter you just read. Many things have transpired which would be too much to record in this book. But I'll share a bit with you so that you can rejoice with me and continue to hold on for your own blessings.

The title of this chapter is key to all that has taken place in my life for the past two years. In my letting go of the familiar and free falling into the hands of God, I took the leap of faith, I became vulnerable. The façade that covered my fears, false sense of prosperity and success, and my seemingly tower of strength dissipated into thin air on my way down, up into God's precious and awesome will.

No one said that this step of faith into the unfamiliar was going to be smooth, enjoyable, nor heavenly. As a matter of fact, as I took the first step to push off, I saw what I was giving up, but not what I would gain. I took a glimpse of the world I had been so long a part of and wondered if when I reached the "net" there would still be financial stability. Ahhh! Leaving the freedom to do what I wanted, when I wanted, seemed just so wrong that the anxiety and fear I felt before taking the leap provided no security for an expected end. Why me? Why now?

Like a child, I JUMPED! Jumped right into— The "jump" was not all that difficult after all. But what was the killer was the not knowing where I would end up. That my friend was the "thud" I imagined hearing if there truly were no net there. It was the angst I began to feel as I writhed in the speculation of "what next." The "do" part of my faith would now have to come alive as the words were really no longer very necessary. No amount of flowery faith words could get me there. The situation needed action.

Leaving my "wonderful" job as teacher and entering into fulltime ministry was not as I expected. It was truly a pull on my faith. Come to think of it, the experience actually resurrected a level of faith that I once had; however, that faith level had been washed over by my own personal financial success. You see, when I had money to provide for whatever I needed, I no longer needed faith—the unwavering assurance that provision would come—as I could easily provide for myself.

Please do not misconstrue what I am saying here. Having the ability to provide for oneself is wonderful, but there needs to be a balance where God is brought in on the decisions when spending our money. When I was financially stable, I did not need to inquire of the Father if I should give this money to this effort, buy this next gadget, go to this event, or save that much. I just did what I wanted because I earned it fair and square.

Now I was in a place of total dependence on God; that meant I was vulnerable. There was no façade left to cover this part of my nakedness. I was left with counting each dollar and appreciating every penny, nickel, dime, and quarter that I had in my purse and apple cider bottles. My vulnerability led me not only to earnestly trust in God, but to patiently wait for Him to come through for me, even in times when I thought He would not be there on time.

With no money coming in, I decided to plan ahead and begin putting together the business end of the ministry. Let me pause here to say that King Solomon was most accurate when he said, *"… but money answereth all things"* (Ecclesiastes 10:19). My situation was calling out to money, but for some reason, "money" wasn't picking up on the call. Perhaps I had the wrong number, but how could I? I dialed correctly: "H-E-L-P M-E L-O-R-D." I had all ten digits, so I don't know what the hold up was?

Again, with no money coming in, I began planning ahead for the ministry. I wrote letters to friends and family announcing this great decision I had made—going into full-time ministry. What that looked like, I didn't know; at least not at that juncture. But I asked that they support me financially if they were led to do so.

That one line I just mentioned—"support me financially"—was erased and retyped several times as I was never one to ask people for anything. Me beg? No sir! I took pride, for the most part, on being sensitive to others' needs and being there for them. But that pride was taken away and now I was left at the mercy of those who believed in what God has called me to do.

Not knowing exactly what I was going to do in full-time ministry was unnerving. Here it is, God tells me to leave my familiar setting and does not give me a map or blueprint of what I am to do. Abraham, I know how you feel, my brother. Vulnerable! Yes, to both man and God. Being vulnerable to God is one thing, but to man? That would require writing another chapter. Ridicule was inevitable, but somehow I had not imagined it coming from some who are members of the household of faith. Yes, I was too naïve in this area as I should have expected it seeing they are a part of my circle of influence.

Shying away from vulnerability is natural. Who wants to expose his or her weakness to anyone? No matter what cultural, ethnic, or religious backgrounds we come from, intrinsically we are taught to be independent of others and not to expect people to do for us what we ought to do for ourselves. But what if that is what God is calling one to do in this season? For me that was obviously apparent, but not wholeheartedly embraced.

In this vulnerability there is a choice—react with strong convictions, hide our weakness, or embrace it with humility and allow it to become that special place in which to have an encounter with God. It is in our place of vulnerability that we feel that the many coats of protective covering are being peeled off to reveal something strange and unusual— our true selves. Yes it feels scary, unpredictable, and comes within inches of being utterly stupid, but something great happens in this place. An encounter with God occurs as we step beyond what is safe into the [un]known.

Into the "known" I stepped—the known of God's promise to take care of me as He has done for centuries for the birds and the lilies of the field—

> *"Consider the ravens: for they neither sow nor reap; which neither have storehouse nor barn; and God feedeth them... If then God so clothe the grass, which is to day in the field, and to morrow is cast into the oven; how much more will he clothe you... But rather seek ye the kingdom of God; and all these things shall be added unto You"* (Luke 12:24, 27-28).

This scripture does not justify one staying home and doing nothing while expecting God to provide for him or her. Rather, it is saying that when we seek after things that are relevant to the kingdom of God and His will, He opens up His window of provision, no matter what channel it comes thru, and blesses us.

Now mind you, I have not read nor seen where God literally came off His throne and physically fed or provided for someone. It is then safe to say that He uses people and other resources to bring hope and help to His children. That is why it is so important that we walk in obedience to His commands as we are His hands and feet to meet the needs of others.

So now back to my vulnerability. I stepped into a place of trust, yet exposure. Sending out those letters meant that I was relying on the love and support of those I thought believed in what I was called to do. About a quarter of those who received my letter responded. The others gave no indication of support in anyway way, shape, or form. There were no nods from them saying,

"I received your letter and will get back with you."

No calls of support as I had expected and no reassurance of,

"I'll be there for you."

I wondered what I had done to cause such poor lack of response. Everyone who knows me can testify that I have always been someone to give. But now, here I stood waiting (with high expectation) to receive. It was now my time to reap some of the benefits of my sacrificial giving. It was my turn to receive after stepping up to the plate in times of emergency. It was now time to reap a harvest from that which I had sown, but it would not be from everyone whom I undoubtedly believed would assist me.

Some laughed at my decision and wondered if I truly heard from God. Others thought I was audacious in expecting people to help me when I made the decision to walk away from my job. Yes, the mean words and laughs came. I felt the pressure of their verbal blows. But, I had entered into a place of faith that would not let me become victim of another person's lack of trust in what God had called me to be and do. Yes, I felt the pain, but somehow God had done something wonderful again.

A wonderful thing occurred in the midst of my pain and waiting. But before I tell you what it is, I need to share this awesome scripture with you: *" For the eyes of the LORD run to and fro throughout the whole earth, to shew himself strong in the behalf of them whose heart is perfect toward him* (2 Chronicles 16:9). This verse is actually saying that my times of weakness show up on God's radar and He reveals Himself in a strong, magnificent way so I will know that it is He alone who could have done this. Now, let us go to the story...

I sat in my office located in the attic of my parent's home and stacked up the bills for the month. When I calculated how much I would need to satisfy the debts, I began to get choked up as I knew I had no where to get all that money. My bills needed over $1,800 to keep the creditors at bay, and I had none of it. Zilch! Nada! Numero zero! Sometimes when I tell this story I let people know that when I obeyed God and went into fulltime ministry, my bills were not informed about the decision.

As I sat at the desk and realized my dilemma, I felt the hot tears come to my eyes. But before they could fall, I stood up, opened my eyes very wide and said, "God, you told me to do this! You told me to do this, and You will not let me be ashamed!"

I felt a settled peace after "reminding" God of the fact that He told me to do this. I meandered my way through the books and paper that decorated my office floor and made it to the couch. I slept there, in my office, for the night.

The next morning, I was awakened with a bang on the attic step.

"Are you decent? Can I come up?" the person asked.

"Sure, I'm still sleepy, but you can come," I responded.

As the person made the ascent up the steep attic stairs, I quickly rubbed my eyes, made myself presentable, and positioned myself to welcome the somewhat unwanted intruder of my solace. It was a holiday and it is customary to sleep until one feels like getting up on those special days that were designated for one thing—doing nothing in my house.

As I tried to shield the early morning sunlight that pierced the two small windows across from my place of rest, I saw the figure of gentleman walking towards me. Before I could say anything that would resemble something like "Couldn't this wait?" he burst the short moment of silence with,

"How are you doing?" he asked as he shifted my magazines to one side and sat down on my make-shift center table.

"I'm okay, just tired," I replied.

Without any long discourse or introductory comments, he said,

"My wife and I believe in what God has called you to do, and we want to support you. Here is something for the ministry," he said with a smile.

Shifting my body to a more comfortable position and wondering "what is this all, about, Lord?" I opened the white envelope to find a check. I realized it was a check from its backside. The front was not yet visible to me, but I was excited just from the makings of what I knew was a check. It truly did not matter if it were for ten dollars or one hundred dollars. It was a check. Money.

"Take it out and look at it," he exclaimed.

As I pulled it from its covering and turned it over, I began to sob immediately. Tears flowed like someone had just turned on the hose to water a much needed patch of grass. I cried so much that the sobs were interrupted by spouts of hyperventilation. It. It. It was a check for six thousand dollars. Never in my life have I ever received so much money in one sitting.

That was just the beginning. God had seen my heart. He knew my desire toward Him was perfect and that was all His radar needed to zone in on my need. Unexpected as it was, the ten digits I dialed a few weeks back was finally answered—"H-E-L-P M-E L-O-R-D."

As I sobbed and thanked the dear brother, he said,

"Here. This is for you to help take care of yourself."

I did not need to look at it as I was already overcome by the first blessing. As I dried my tears long enough to open and read the check, I realized that something I said the night before had set things into motion.

"Two thousand dollars just for me," I said with tears running down my face as I hyperventilated as a child who just received a vicious spanking.

No words could explain this great act of God. Of course I thanked this Spirit-led man of God profusely, but it seemed insignificant to the magnitude of what he and his wife had given.

That final statement I made before going to sleep had sealed my position. Although the words I said to God were not exactly that of the Shunammite woman in the 4th chapter of 2 Kings, they embodied its sentiments. In her dilemma she said, "It is well." The thing that mattered most to her had just died, but her response to the questions was, "It is well."

Lord, I see the situation, but…

I know my child is dead, but…

I know it's not the time to visit the man of God, but…

I know I don't have a job, but…

True, my bills are more than I can pay, but…

Like her, I had summoned heaven to respond to my faith by putting the responsibility on God. I was walking in obedience to His voice and my weakness of pride— always providing for myself—was exposed. I could no longer rely on doing whatever I wanted for myself because I had the money. I was at His mercy, His love, and His care.

I do not know what conversations went on in heaven as I slept during the night, but my imagination tells me that a decision was made long before I took the leap of faith. It only needed my words and action to bring it to pass. What I said to God that night released provision on my behalf. It was always there. It only needed a word of confidence and an act of faith from me for it to be released, to materialize.

What an encounter! God made Himself known to me as my Jehovah-Jireh. The covenant-keeping God lovingly lifted my eyes to see Him as provider in total. The revelation of Himself in the midst of my weakness provided the foundation I needed to trust Him from that point on. Could there be another opportunity of need that I would trust if He would come through for me? Yes, many more situations came my way. But in reflection, I found out that I still held on to this one thing—If He brings me to it, He will take me through it.

Yes, I have had some close calls where I thought this was going to be the test that would prove my faith futile. But somehow, God has kept me up and stabilized my footing in Him. He has given me opportunities to develop a trust that says, "I know that God is especially interested and invested in my welfare." Developing that trust was birthed out of my vulnerability. As frightening as it may seem, this path promises to pay more than it requires us to give.

Now what is so special about vulnerability? Well, from my experiences, it is oh so painfully real! In being vulnerable, we are sometimes tricked by our fears and want to run into hiding. We shriek at the thought of someone seeing our weaknesses and finding out that the persona we reflect is truly not all what it is made out to be.

The aspect of vulnerability I love most is the opportunity to meet God in the most unlikely places: in our weaknesses, our fears; the lonely times when no one wants to associate with us because of our unpopular decisions; the place of rejection and pain; the times of doubt and discouragement; and the times when we are faced with (metaphorically) our hands up and our pants down. It is in these times that we encounter God by experiencing His love, mercy, encouragement, and provision.

I have started off on a great path that many have traveled. I have stepped out of my comfort zone into a place of uncertainty without a map of where I am going and what I will in all actuality do.

I wonder what is around the corner. Hmmmmm…

REFLECTION ON LESSONS LEARNED

←*←*←*←*←*←*←

Being vulnerable is not as bad as it seems. It actually opened me up to other levels of weakness I never thought existed. Did it scare me? No, not really. Initially I thought, "God, you know about all these "yucky" areas in me and still love me? Why did You take such a risk in using me?"

Sounds funny my asking God those questions, but I was genuinely moved by the strength of His love for me even though He knew my weaknesses. Realizing the love God has for me amidst His knowledge of my insufficiencies, there is a sense of genuine compassion I feel when someone is in need, and yes, the needs vary. In essence, when we are aware of our own weaknesses, we become more tolerant of others' shortcomings, more ready to forgive an injury because of the pain we inflicted on another out of our own woundedness, more sensitive to the needs of others because of our place of lack, and we are more prone to laughing at our mistakes because we know it's not the end of the road.

Truly, the times of vulnerability were worth the pain because of the many opportunities I had sweet and invigorating encounters with God. The experiences are priceless, but I'm willing to share some of the lessons learned along the way:

- **Trusting in the Father's care is the cure for anxiety.** I can understand why people sometime do "stupid" things when their backs are against the wall and there is no where else to turn. Imagine being threatened with losing your house, a car, or apartment because you are behind on your payments. What a place to be in and no one to help. Anxiety sets in and various thoughts begin to swirl around in your head. You try every possible avenue to bring reconciliation to the problem, but there is none. Trust has just taken a flying leap out the window and so you re left with only the problem.

  This sets up the perfect scenario for God to move on your behalf. I learned that when my efforts fail, trusting the Father is all I have left to do. This trust puts us in alignment with His will. Problems will come; they are part of life, but the Word of God says, *"Casting all your care upon him; for he careth for you"* (I Peter 5:7). Basically, when your friends do not come through for you, He cares. When the bill collector does not want to hear your reason for being late with your payment, He cares. When your back is against the wall, He cares.

  Trusting will release your tension. It will set your mind at ease, change your perspective, and push you beyond the threshold of defeat to hope. It will release the faith needed to affect change on your behalf.

- **Do not blame God for your problems.** The enemy always uses our times of "darkness" to curse the Light. Jesus is always there with us whether or not we can see or feel Him. Our first response should be to trust Him knowing that He has our best interest at heart. You may feel the need to ask Him questions like, "What do I do now, Lord?" or, "Why is this happening to me?" It's okay. He does not mind us asking Him questions.

God is the greatest example of a father, so why should He not expect us to question what is going on. Jesus may not answer all of the questions or even come through when you think He needs to, but know this, [and I put emphasis here], He cares and wants to see the best come through for you. Sometimes waiting is for our development in Him. He really does not gain anything from us when we complain through the process. He truly wants us to make the most of every situation. Try it and see what happens.

- **When you receive, give!** The money that was given to me helped to establish the business end of the ministry. I also used part of it to sow a seed in a new ministry; support a youth group of an affiliating church; buy gifts for underprivileged women in the rural areas of Jamaica, to send along with Bibles and other Christian literature to the island; gave some of it to support other ministries in the United States; and was led to sow several hundred dollars in the lives of other individuals. As a result of my giving, I continued to receive even after the eight thousand dollar blessing.

- **Forgive those who do not understand your position in God.** I shared with you that I was laughed at and talked about when I left my job for full-time ministry. Well, although their words did hurt for a little while, I had to shift to a place of forgiveness. I could not go on and be healthy in my spirit with the baggage of anger, resentment, and bitterness. Yes, I trusted these folks; some of them were what one would consider friends. But what a waste my leap of faith would have been if I had given in to my hurt and disappointment? Surely, I would not be able to give you these helpful nuggets to support you along the way.

In all of this, though, God was teaching me unconditional love and perfecting in me gifts that He had deposited in my spirit. So go ahead, release the people you have carried for so long in your heart. Free yourself from their lack of vision into what God has planned for your life. Grow from the experience and watch Him turn your situation around to bring Himself glory and you an expected end.

Friend, God is creating an opportunity to reveal Himself to you during your time of disappointment. Remember, give yourself the opportunity to show up on God's radar, so He can "show Himself strong..." on your behalf. He's excited about you and the path He has ordained for your feet. Take that leap and fall down, down, down into the presence of His everlasting arms, up into glory.

CHAPTER SIXTEEN

"BE STILL AND KNOW..."

*"I will take time to quiet my mind, to rest
my heart and refresh my soul."*
—Anonymous

Okay, God. I am ready to know now. I am ready to begin doing what you need for me to do. Just show me and I'll follow. Sounds reasonable? Sure it does, especially when we have given up all to enter into what He has designed for us. Here it is, we step out on faith and are following God closely, but somewhere along the path, we miss His presence. We take a wrong turn without His guidance, or we simply are not patient enough to see Him pointing us to the next level, the next dimension.

Here it is. At least a couple months had gone by, and I began to have thoughts of seeking employment to augment the few donations that came in periodically. I was only going to substitute teach for a little while. Nothing great or permanent would be entertained by me seeing God had called me into fulltime ministry.

I toyed with the idea as my parents thought that that was what I would do to help ends meet for myself. I could easily set my own schedule and still do the Lord's work: be an itinerant minister, write biblical literature; teach Bible class and donate time to a ministry that meets the needs of the homeless in downtown Washington, D.C. I could still do all these things and teach as a substitute in Maryland schools for a little while.

I had this all figured out. After some pondering of the idea, I received a phone call from a good friend in Fairfax County. She said that there was a long-term substitute position available and it was mine if I wanted the job. Still to this day, I cannot tell you why I did not say "yes" immediately. I know it was God leading me, but that is because hindsight is 20/20.

"I'll get back with you in a few days to let you know of my decision," I, with reservation, responded. There was a burst of joy that exuded the atmosphere and then, without notice, this unsettling feeling of anxiety came over me. I felt like I had done something wrong that would forever affect my life. What generated this mysterious feeling? Why was such wonderful news overshadowed by gloom and an air of imminent catastrophe? It was as if a perfectly good and exciting train ride had been interrupted by an unannounced engine headed in the same direction of the train. Danger seemed to be looming nearby, but why?

I wrestled with making the decision to take the position. Part of me had begun to imagine the end of my calculating the prices of things I picked up in the store just to make sure I had enough money to purchase the items. I could go back to being totally independent, getting anything I wanted at anytime; at least some things. What a beautiful thought that was, but it was brief. The unsettling feeling in my stomach had me wondering, "Does God not want me to do substitute teaching?"

A few days later, I visited with my brother Aldean, his wife, and their two children. Julianne asked how I was doing so far. I shared with her the awesome prospect of teaching again and the weird feeling I was also having. Being as in tuned to the Spirit as she is, Julianne immediately began to minister to me.

"What did God tell you to do when you left your job in Fairfax?" she asked.

"He said He has called me into full-time ministry," I responded.

"So why are you wrestling with taking this job? Will you not be going back into what He has called you from?" she asked.

"I guess so... I don't know!" I quipped.

"If you don't know what to do, then you need to be still until He speaks to you," Julianne replied.

Be still! Who wants to be still when life is constantly moving, progressing, making leaps, and bounds? I have always been active and physically doing something. But now here I was at home writing biblical literature and sending out letters to organizations that fund persons in full-time ministry. Being still was not something that was strange to me. I had already experienced being still, somewhat.

"Julianne, you don't understand where I am right now..." I professed.

The next words that flowed from her lips were so arresting that all I could do was say,

"Yes, Lord!"

She began to share the story of Jesus with His disciples and the storm in St. John 6:16-21. After Jesus fed the 5,000 with two fish and five loaves of bread, He went to the mountain alone, and His disciples decided to go down to the sea and wait for Him there. But something spectacular happened:

> *16 That evening his disciples went down to the shore to wait for him. 17 But as darkness fell and Jesus still hadn't come back, they got into the boat and headed*

out across the lake toward Capernaum. [18] Soon a gale swept down upon them as they rowed, and the sea grew very rough. [19] They were three or four miles out when suddenly they saw Jesus walking on the water toward the boat. They were terrified, [20] but he called out to them, "I am here! Don't be afraid." [21] Then they were eager to let him in, and immediately the boat arrived at their destination! (LB).

Did you see it? Neither did I at first. I only realized it after Julianne expounded upon the verse and made it relevant to my situation.

Here it is. The disciples had just seen Jesus do a marvelous and incredible miracle. It was not their first experience, but this seemed to have been one of the most miraculous of events. Can you imagine their conversation on the way back to the seashore?

"Did you see that, John…and all that food from one boy's lunch? Incredible!" Peter probably said.

They could probably still taste the flavor of that bread and fish in their mouths. This was a personal experience, not just one they saw with their eyes or heard from a neighbor. They went to the boat with an awesome testimony of Jesus' incredible power. And so there they waited for Him. They watched as the sun disappeared behind the shadows of darkness that had now begun to come over this seaport town of Galilee. Certainly they wondered what was taking Jesus so long. Surely they waited eagerly to find out how that great miracle was done. They probably wanted to ask,

"Jesus, did you know that that boy was going to bring lunch?"

"Did you know that you would have to feed all these people with it?"

Questions. Questions. Questions. They must have had several carefully orchestrated questions churning in their minds while waiting for the Master to come. But what was the hold up? It was getting late now.

"Let's push off," one of them must have said.

"But the Master is not here yet, maybe we should wait?" another plead.

Probably some more minutes went by before the first ore hit the shallow ground of the seabed to give the boat a push. But push off they did. They seemed to have already picked out the course of travel they would take. Now they headed for Capernaum without the Master aboard the boat.

Darkness had fallen and the tide began to rise. Near the shore there was no indication of a storm brewing, but here they were faced with a storm less than two or three miles after they had pushed off from shore. Without obvious notice, a windstorm came swooping in and the water they trusted near shore was now their fierce enemy.

They began to row furiously. Nothing seemed to be working. They rowed, looked out toward the distant shore to see if the Master had come, but it was too dark now. No one or no thing could be seen in the darkness as the waters came crashing against the boat, tossing the disciples back and forth, up and down.

Surely they must have been terrified by the strong wind and gushing waves. They rowed and rowed when suddenly they saw the Master walking on the water towards them. Fear gripped their hearts. Suddenly, through all that noise of rain, wind, waves, and the battling of ores against the side of the boat, Jesus called out to them.

"I am here! Don't be afraid."

Those calming and reassuring words from the Master traveled through the chaos of the storm and reached their ears in time to settle their fears. There was probably a release of,

"It will be okay now, the Master is here." Their actions spoke it, for they eagerly brought Him aboard.

The key in this story is not that Jesus came aboard the boat and everything was now alright. The true essence of this story is that their impatience with the Master led them into a storm. Did you get that? Waiting on the Master took up too much of their time. Waiting was an issue. Besides, it was getting dark and the need to get to the next destination was on their minds.

When Julianne brought this to my attention, I realized that I was not being patient with God regarding my new profession—full-time ministry. I needed money as funds were getting low, and I could not readily adjust to the inconsistency of having and then not having. Taking that long-term substitute position looked mighty fine with those factors in place. But what would lie in the path ahead? My taking the job would resemble my getting in the boat and pushing off into—

Her exegetical explanation of this story was profound and convicting. I left her presence with a settled peace that my discomfort was not based on fear, but that it was the Holy Spirit's way of letting me know that this was not God's will. When I arrived home and reflected on the experience, the Holy Spirit reminded me that the Lord had said that I was not to seek employment until He had released me to do so. I FORGOT! My perspective was truly clouded by my need for independence.

And here I was being tried in the area of waiting, even when I was walking with a lapsed memory. And wait I did. I continued writing, compiling biblical literature, and putting the ministry together. It was in my waiting that He made Himself known to me in a supernatural way.

Provider. Mechanic. Doctor. Banker. God became all these and more to me as I remained in the "still" position. Psalm 46:10 says, *"Be still and know that I am God: I will be exalted among the heathen, I will be exalted in the earth."* Many times we do not give God a chance to be exalted before our friends, co-workers, family, and strangers because we do not wait. Being still when everything around you says you should be moving is not an easy feat. But it must be done for a greater glory.

It was good that I did wait. The path that God ordained for my feet was one I did not consider. Being in seminary was not a part of the "deal" when I left the Detention Center. But that was what God had in mind, along with a few other things.

I attended a conference on the campus of a religious university. I did not know it at the time as we stayed at a hotel on the campus. I ventured to ask what this beautiful place was. "Regent University," a passerby overhearing my conversation with a friend responded. He began to explain the aspects of the university to me. My curiosity peaked, and I began to gather pamphlets and any information I could get my hands on regarding the school.

Without going through a long story, I applied and was accepted. You know what? I want to share a little bit with you regarding what led to my attending the university. I was attending a worship conference hosted by Keith and Michelle Duncan of His Call Ministries. It was called the Throne Zone Worship Conference, and by the end of the event, you knew that that was exactly where you had been the whole time — in the presence of God around His throne.

During the conference, I was prompted by the Holy Spirit to give a special offering on two separate nights. I needed not to worry where I was going to get the money from since I had just received $1500 dollars from a lovely couple as a seed offering. However, I had already made plans for the money — shopping, shopping, and shopping. But God had other plans.

Needless to say, I gave all of it. No, it was not easy to give up all that money to a ministry that I had just been introduced to, but my obedience to the Father was more important. My not too distant past experiences of trusting and being obedient to Him then seeing the results were what fueled my decision to listen.

I later realized that the ground on which I sowed that $1500 would reap a harvest. I applied for and received a partial scholarship from the University. It was more than I had given. Again, God proved Himself to me.

Waiting. Who wants to wait? Who wants to be still? So much seems to go by when we are waiting. But being still and waiting for direction from God is tantamount to our success. There are so many pitfalls, failures, disappointments, and tragedies we can avoid if we truly wait.

Waiting helps to bring clarity to things. His voice becomes sharper to our spiritual ears. Our eyes are focused on the things that matter. We can step back from the busyness of life and see the real picture of where we are and the direction God wants to take us. Remember the story we just read? Take a look at it again. The Bible does not tell us that the storm ceased. But we can conjecture that it did because they reached their destination immediately after Jesus entered the boat.

That's powerful. "What's powerful?" you may be asking. Well, I'll tell you—the fact that they reached their destination <u>immediately</u> after Jesus entered the boat. It was storming and the waves were tumultuous before Jesus' ascent into the boat. But when He entered, a perfect calm was experienced. An immediate arrival to their destination came.

When we wait, the path to our destination can be shortened; we are able to obtain and do things that would have required a longer journey, a lengthier process. My mentioning that to you brings me to a childhood dream I had, but thought I could never see or even experience.

As a youth in middle school I had very high ambitions for myself, even though I knew many were unreachable and even impossible by man's standards and rules. I had my hopes set on attending Oxford University. Yes, I did, but I knew my ethnic, social, and economical background would put me in a "don't even think about it" category. Well, several years later, my childhood dream came to fruition. Through Regent University, I was able to study Religion and Politics at Oxford University for part of the summer in 2006. What a great honor that was. Because I waited, I was able to walk through a door that was prepared for me from before the desire to go to seminary existed.

Waiting sometimes is still a bit of a trouble for me, depending on the reason for the wait. But I have learned that the process is good for me. What waiting does for us is bring out the issues, the inhibitions and the "yuck" that would hold us back from achieving what God has in store for us. We get a clear picture of ourselves—that we are miniscule in comparison to His magnificent splendor—and we grow to appreciate the relationship that is birthed out of our waiting. We also get to see that we are forever indebted to Him during our seasons of waiting.

God wants to exalt Himself in our waiting. He wants us to see Him. See Him in His strength, true beauty, and holiness. God desires to bring us to a place of peace and an expected end, but we must learn to wait. I encourage you to step back and see God magnify Himself in your life.

Stop!
Rest!
Be still!
And know…

THE CONCLUSION

"It aint over 'til God says so!" —Anonymous

L ife. Life. Life. What a thought!
God designed life in such a way that only He can fully understand all the aspects of it. But each day, He allows us to see a glimpse of what it contains in contrast to Him. Disappointments will come, yet, we will experience joy and happiness. There will be confusion at times, and we'll experience rejection. But that is what life is all about—experiences.

The road of life is not going to be easy all the time. I stand here in agreement on that. But as you travel up the mountain, please know that there are seasons of rain, snow, sunshine, warmth, wind, storm, and rest. In all of these seasons, God brings about a change for His glory and for a wonderful expected end for us.

Death comes in some seasons. Life springs up in others. There is even a season where things are dormant to the point where we wonder if life still exists. But if you and I can just hold on until Spring, stay focused until the dark skies roll away, remain faithful until the pain of your storm rides its way through, and stay close under the mighty arm of God until we feel the security of His love, then we will see as He sees. We will hear as He hears. We will talk as He talks. And we will feel as He feels.

Just think about it. All the strength we thought was gone was being fortified in our stillness. The silence of God that we thought meant He no longer cared for us has built our senses up to recognize Him in everything around us. The stand we took when others thought we were foolish has now multiplied to build us a stronger foundation of courage and defense.

The times we gave, though others mistook it for weakness, have planted seeds to bring us a larger harvest. And in the times when we wait to see our expected end, God magnifies Himself and gives us more than we ever imagined.

"Hallelujah! Glory to God!"

When I started this book, I had no idea where the path that God had ordained for my feet would lead me. But through the struggles and triumphs, I had the awesome experience of seeing how God made it all come together to paint the picture of my future—ministry. I am a mouthpiece of God to the nations.

No, I was not to be a lawyer. I was being groomed, fashioned, purged, refined, and tailor-made for that one thing in which I would glorify God. Yes, it took some time. Yes, I lost some friends along the way. Most assuredly I walked sometime hoping that many of the challenges I was facing were horrible dreams from which I could easily awake. Of course I reflect and wonder what my life would have been like if I had not obeyed. And no, I do not resent, hate, or have any bitter feelings towards people or the process. As a matter of fact, those two factors—people and the process—helped to get me where I am today.

I am thriving in the presence of God because I am planted by His rivers of water. My roots are deep in His will, and the fruits that grow on my tree come in their season. I refuse to allow the lessons learned in the past to become ineffective in my present and future state. I need my fruits to help feed the body of Christ. I need my fruits to go forth and feed the hungry nations that are dying without hope in Jesus Christ. Yes, my fruits come in their seasons to help bring deliverance to nations and people.

So what do I do now to maintain my stability in Christ? I rest in Him and allow my steps to be ordered by His hand. I maximize my experiences as they are part of the processing of my destiny. I also reflect often as a form of checks and balances in order to retain a healthy perspective on things.

Here's a wonderful quote a good friend of mine gave me that I know will help: "Whatever you feed will grow, and whatever you starve will die." Feeding the hurt, pain, and disappoint of the past will only stunt your growth. You will not be able to move forward in the purpose God has designed for you. And you will live an unfulfilled life.

So go ahead. Allow Him to stretch you and to take you to a place that is unfamiliar to prove His love and admiration of you.

Reach out and touch the soft wind of His Spirit. Give Him access to you and allow Him to create the true person you were meant to be. Come now and experience the fresh aroma of His presence as He "Springs" up into your life while you are living on the mountain.

I'LL SEE YOU...?

I pray this book was a blessing. I pray that you gleaned enough information to push you in the direction and destiny God has ordained for your life. I truly enjoyed sharing a little of myself with you, a member of "my" family.

You may have carried me into your living room, the subway, the bathroom, the car, the deck, the bus station, and even the garage. I might have been misplaced under the seat of your couch or nearly gotten burned by the fire from the grill. I may have been left in your backpack for a few days. Your husband's boots may have slept on me overnight under the bed. The cat may have scratched my title, and I may have been used as lighter fuel for the backyard barbeque, or possibly bent and torn around the edges by your teething 7-month-old daughter. But I thank you for letting me spend some time with you through the pages of this book.

May God bless and preserve that mighty thing He has started in you. You are special to Him. <u>Any</u> and <u>everything</u> that happens to you matters to Him. You are not here by chance, but by design. Your existence, no matter how you came about, was ordained from before creation. You are destined for greatness! Therefore, live out your purpose, live out your destiny, and live out the will of the Father in your life. He's waiting on you and I am counting on you.

God loves and cares for you. I love and care about you, too, 'cause you're a member of "my" family, the family of God. Be blessed!

ABOUT THE AUTHOR

Hewlette Pearson, motivational speaker, teacher, and author, is a vivacious and eloquent woman of God who enjoys sharing the gospel of Jesus Christ in a practical way. She has been teaching and preaching the Word of God for over 18 years. The anointing of God is upon her life and is seen in her delivery of the word and operation in the prophetic ministry.

A native of Kingston, Jamaica, Hewlette Pearson migrated to the United States with her family and took up residency in Washington, D.C. Having the support of her parents and three brothers, she has accomplished much both in the religious and secular fields. Ordained into the ministry in December 2000, she has traveled within the United States and other countries to minister. Her common sense, down to earth delivery of the Word, and sense of humor captivates audiences wherever she goes.

Currently, Hewlette is pursuing a Master of Divinity degree at Regent University, Virginia Beach, Virginia. Hewlette Pearson has earned degrees from the University of the District of Columbia and Johns Hopkins University. She is also a member of Phi Delta Kappa, an international fraternity of educators, and is listed in Who's Who Historical Society's *2001-2002 International Who's Who of Professional Educators.*

As founder of Hewlette Pearson Ministries, Inc., she is dedicated to declaring God's kingdom existence and objectives, and is determined to bring salvation and the love of Jesus Christ to the peoples of the world. The Holy Spirit has endowed her with many gifts and talents; however, she believes strongly in being led of the Holy Spirit in every aspect of her life. For Hewlette Pearson, ministering is her gift, but God is her passion.

<u>Mailing Information</u>
Hewlette Pearson
P.O. Box 11315
Takoma Park, MD 20913
<u>www.HPearsonMinistries.org</u>

MINISTRIES OF INFLUENCE

†**Keith Duncan** is a consummate worshiper. His ministry of worship has helped to birth in me an insatiable desire for the presence of God. I am honored to be a partner in his ministry as I am constantly refreshed, renewed, and energized after attending his "soaking in the presence of God" Summits and Throne Zone Worship Conferences.

Keith and his wife, Michele, are the founders of His Call Ministries. HCM endeavors to rally cities together breaking down racial and denominational barriers through the medium of music. Keith has organized events from the annual Throne Zone Worship Conference, the Hampton Coliseum, to regional worship conferences, as well as hosting Nights of Worship. Currently, he is serving as the worship leader at the Inspiration Networks (INSP), located in Charlotte, NC, and travels teaching, training, and leading in worship. His duties at INSP include guest worship leading on "The Inspiration Today" show and music director / worship leader for INSP Camp-meetings. Keith has also worked with Ron Kenoly, Benny Hinn, Morris Cerullo, 4-Him, John Tesh, Avalon, Judy Jacobs, and Alicia Williams, just to name a few.

As an itinerate minister, he travels two to three weekends a month speaking or leading others into the presence of

God through worship. Keith's heart is for intimate worship; simply stated, "Worship is on the Father's Heart". He is most concerned about helping people to understand true worship and how it can impact their daily lives and even transform cities.

Contact Information:
His Call Ministries
P.O. Box 49307
Charlotte, N.C. 28277
803.547.2210
www.HisCall.org

†**T.D. Jakes**, founder and senior pastor of The Potter's House, Dallas, Texas, is a man of great spiritual stature. He has been instrumental in providing "on time" messages to sustain me through many of the storms that I encountered on my way up the "Mountain." His god-inspired sermons helped to bring the spiritual healing I needed, many times, and I am encouraged by his indefatigable spirit towards the work of God.

Contact Information:
T. D. Jakes Ministries
P.O. Box 5390
Dallas, Texas 75208
800.BISHOP.2
www.TDJakes.org

†**Bishop Charles Lewis** is founder and senior pastor of For His Glory Church, Camp Springs, MD. The first time I sat under his teaching, I felt the presence of God doing an inner work in the broken areas of my life. I'll never forget that day

because I was in so much emotional pain, but no one knew. God used him to bring healing to my wounded spirit. The prophetic anointing on his life is evident as he goes forth in ministering the gospel to "the poor, bringing healing to the brokenhearted, preaching deliverance to the captives...and setting at liberty them that are bruised..." He is truly a spiritual giant in the body of Christ.

Contact Information:
For His Glory Church
P.O. Box 30526
Washington, D.C. 20030-0526
202.561.3068

†**Prophetess Juanita Bynum**, an anointed woman of God, has been an inspiration to me in ministry. Her deep desire and relentless pursuit of the presence of God through the means of prayer encouraged me to seek God's face continually. There is never a week that goes by that I do not play her "A Piece of My Passion" compact discs. The songs have helped to create and maintain the atmosphere I needed as I lay in prayer at Jesus' feet. I have also received encouragement and wisdom from her ministry of the Word. She continues to inspire me.

Contact Information:
Juanita Bynum Ministries
P. O. Box 939,
Waycross, GA 31501.
912.287.0032
www.JuanitaBynum.com

†**Aldean and Julianne Pearson**, ministers of reconciliation and inspiration, are true-to-life examples of faith in action. Their indefatigable spirit towards educating and equipping others with the necessary tools to live victorious lives is a testament to the mighty hand of God upon their life. Their daily walk of faith has helped to build my faith in the promises of God. The counsel I received from Aldean and Julianne Pearson, during some of the difficult times in my life, helped to keep me focused on what truly mattered—walking the path toward my destiny. True ministers you are!

Contact Information:
LĪVE! Ministries
9427 Monroe Street #816
Crown Point, IN 46307

†**Pastor Margaret Gibson** is founder and senior pastor of City on the Hill Church. She is a woman of wisdom and GREAT faith. I am inspired by her deep passion for souls and the tenacious spirit she has in carrying out God's kingdom objectives. Challenges, disappointments, and obstacles have come her way, but her love for God and what He has called her to do in His kingdom are the building blocks of the foundation on which she stands, daily. I am encouraged by her fortitude and wisdom.

Contact Information:
City on the Hill Church
P.O. Box 2913
Stafford, Virginia 22555
www.CityOnTheHill.net

†**Pastor Samuel W. Carson, Sr.**, a man of faith and integrity, is senior pastor of Shiloh Church of God 7th Day, Hyattsville, MD. For over thirty years, he has been a source of encouragement to me. It was he who saw the gifts that God placed within me and began to call them forth by challenging me to study the Word and to go forth in my pursuit of seminary training. Pastor Carson stepped over the barrier of gender-divide and began to use me in capacities that were not "normal" for female believers. This spoke volumes to the trust he had for what God had deposited inside of me. I will forever be indebted to him for helping me take note of my unrealized potential. His walk of integrity inspires me.

Contact Information:
Shiloh Church of God, 7th Day
5701 Eastern Avenue
Hyattsville, MD 20782
301.559.5262

Printed in the United States
71362LV00002B/136-999